SPECTRUM®

Math

Grade 1

Published by Spectrum®
an imprint of Carson-Dellosa Publishing LLC
Greensboro, NC

Spectrum®
An imprint of Carson-Dellosa Publishing LLC
P.O. Box 35665
Greensboro, NC 27425 USA

ISBN 978-0-7696-3691-7

15-266137811

Table of Contents Grade 1

Table of Contents, continued

NAME ______________________

Lesson 1.1 Counting 0 through 4

zero	one	two	three	four
0	1	2	3	4

Circle the number.

0 1 2 3 4

0 1 2 3 4

0 1 2 3 4

0 1 2 3 4

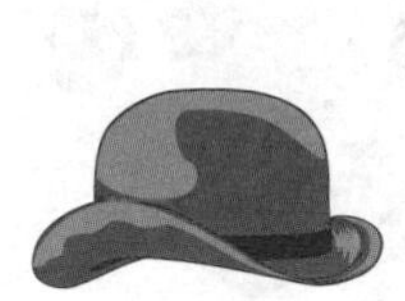

0 1 2 3 4

0 1 2 3 4

NAME ____________________

Lesson 1.2 Counting 5 through 7

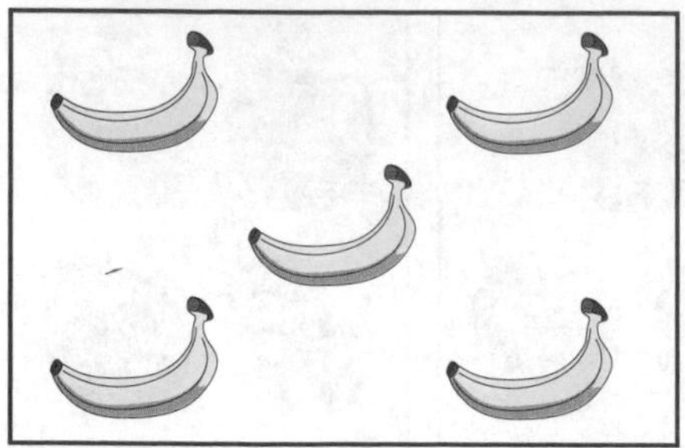

five

5

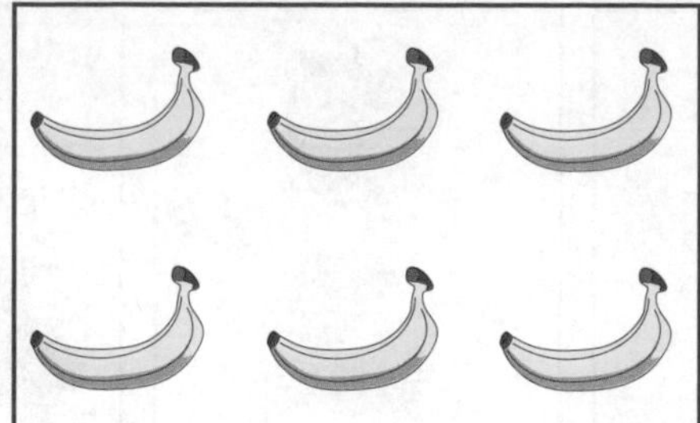

six

6

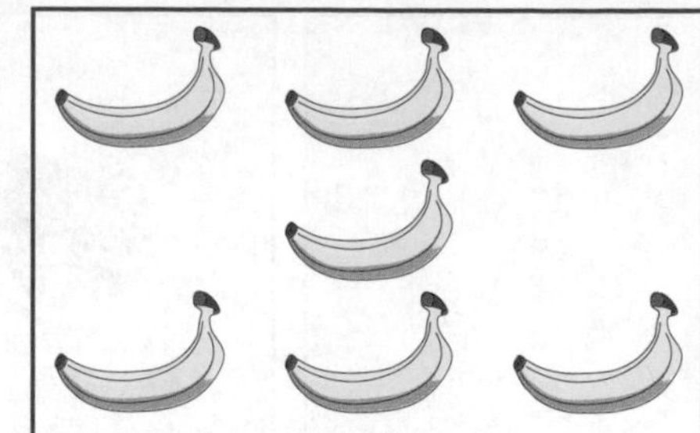

seven

7

Circle the number.

5 6 7

5 6 7

5 6 7

5 6 7

5 6 7

5 6 7

Lesson 1.3 Counting 8 through 10

eight

8

nine

9

ten

10

Circle the number.

8 9 10

8 9 10

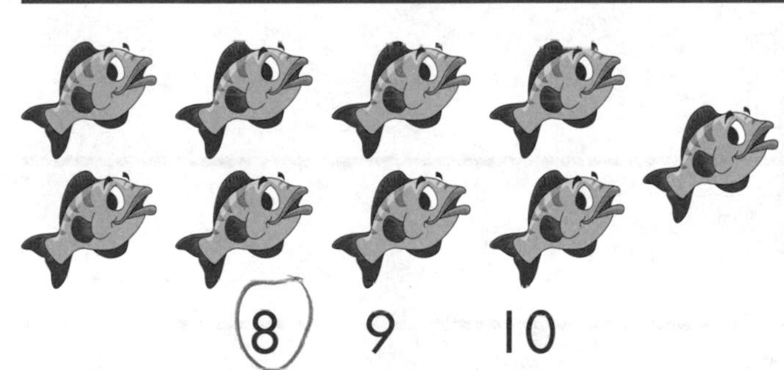

8 9 10

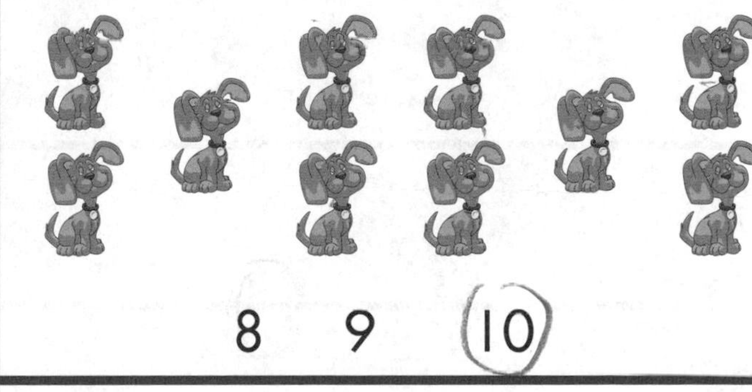

8 9 10

8 9 10

8 9 10

NAME ______________________

Lesson 1.4 Counting 0 through 10

Read the number. Color that many balloons.

0 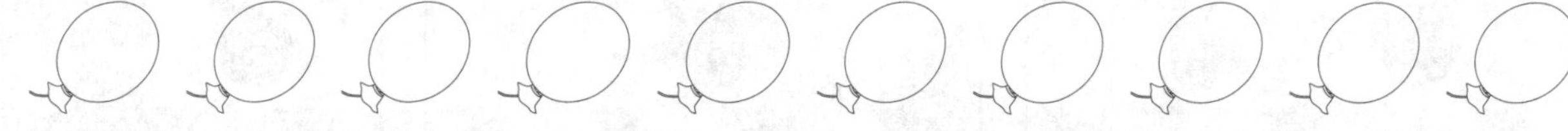

1 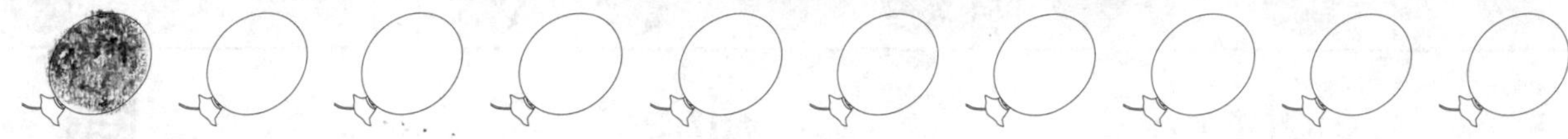

2 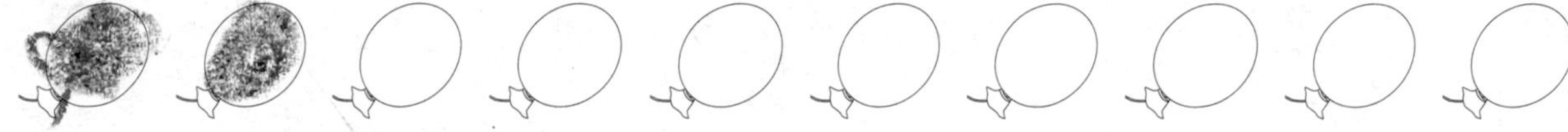

3 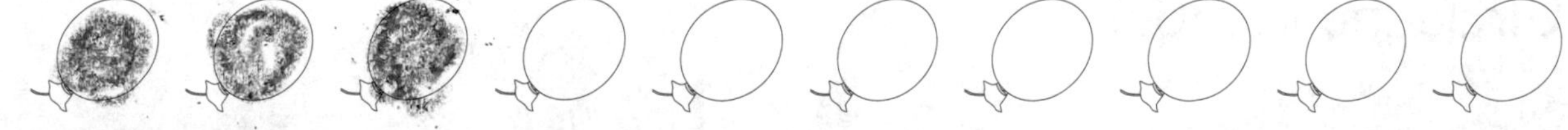

4 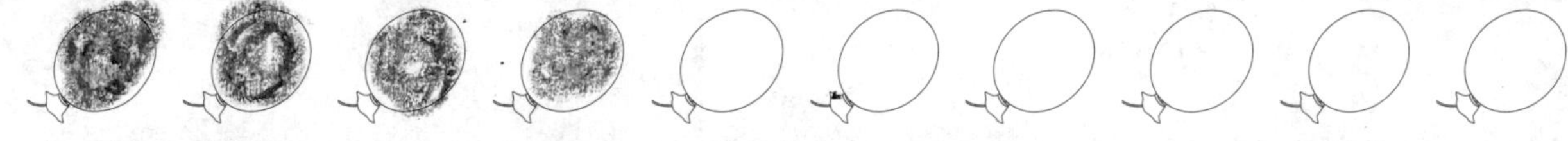

5 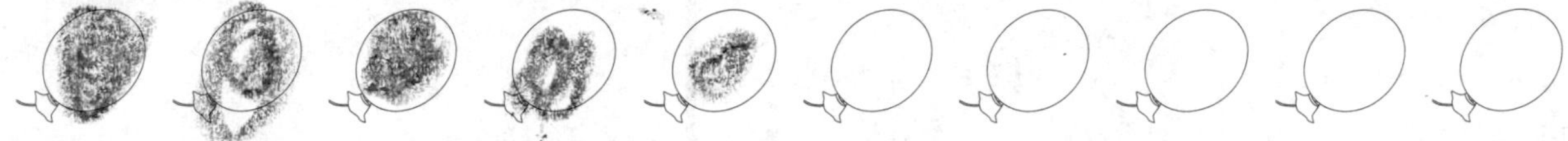

6 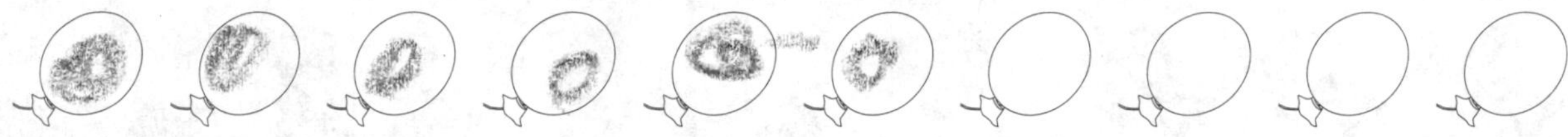

7 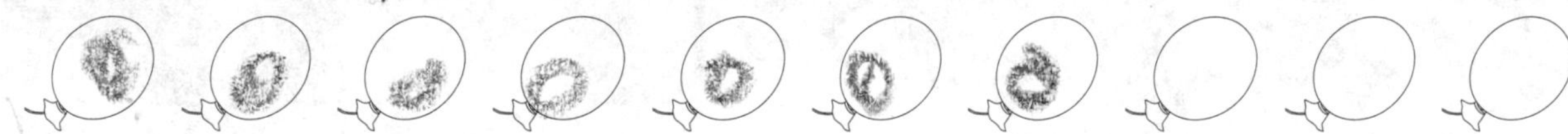

8 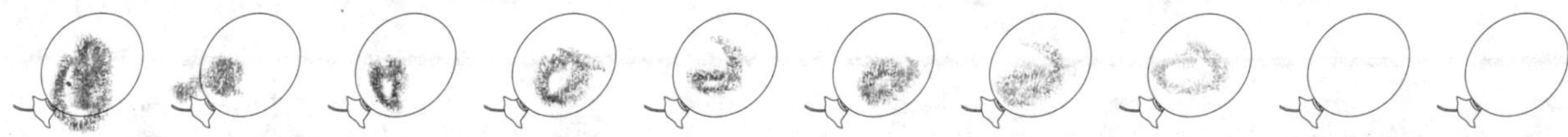

9 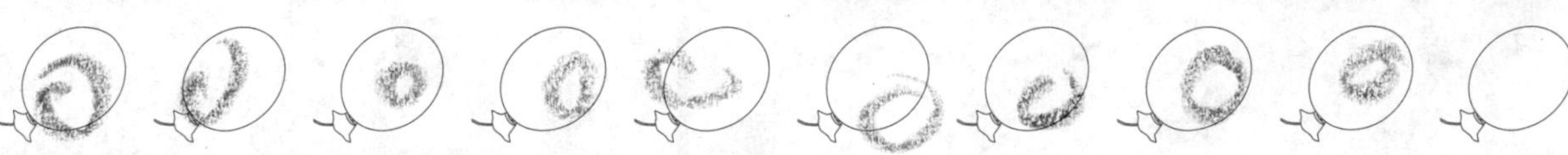

10 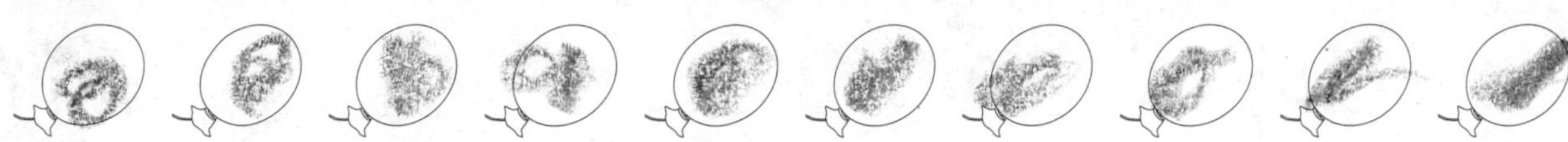

NAME ______________________

Lesson 1.5 Counting and Writing 0 through 10

Count the .
Say the number.
Write the word for that number.

6 six	4
2	7
5	10
8	3

NAME ____________________

Lesson 1.5 Counting and Writing 0 through 10

Count how many.
Write the number.

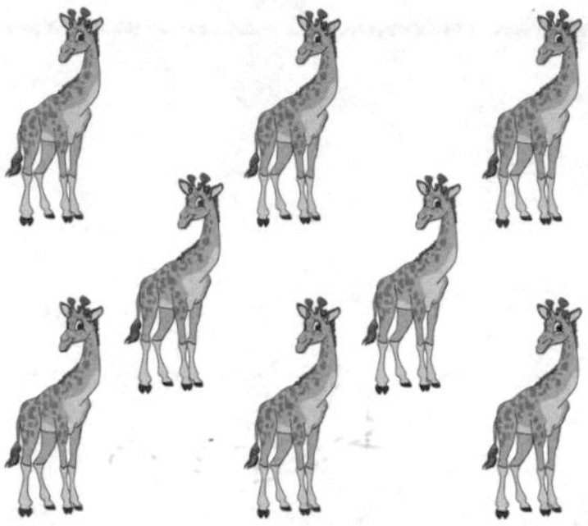

8

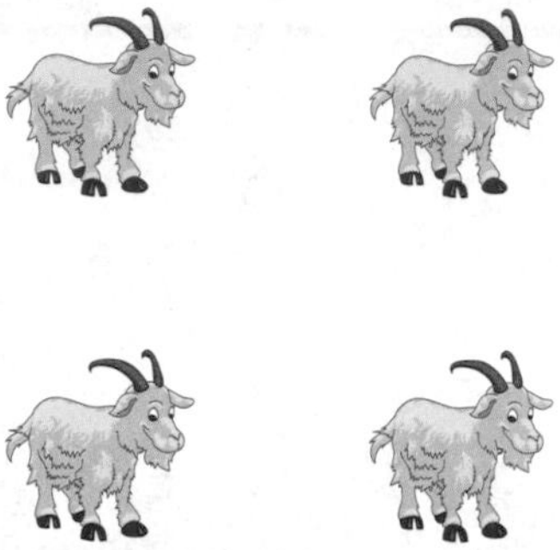

4

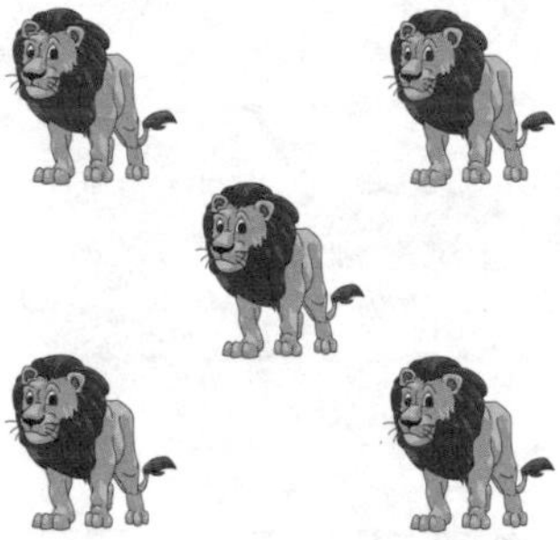

5

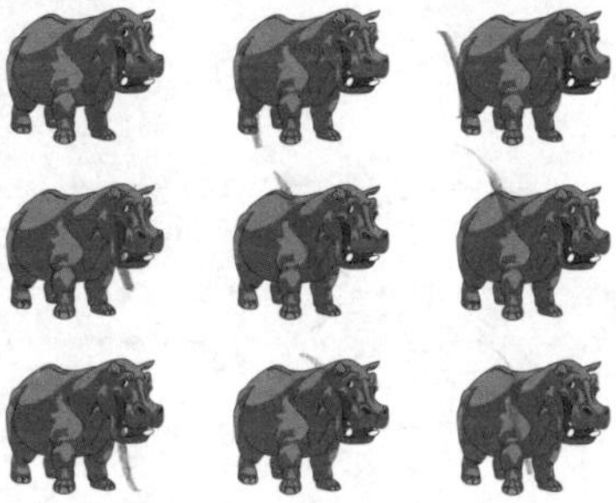

9

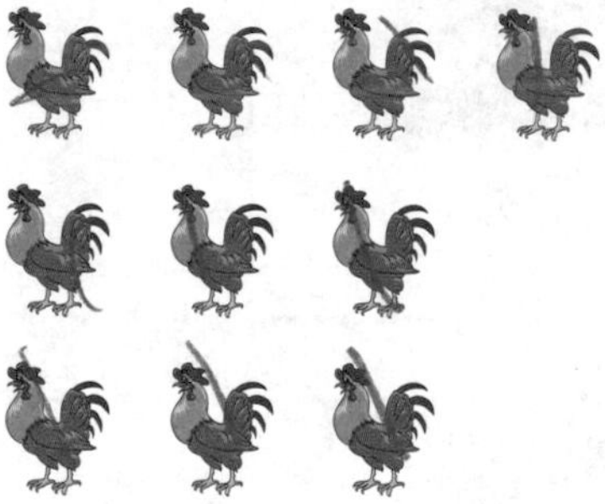

10

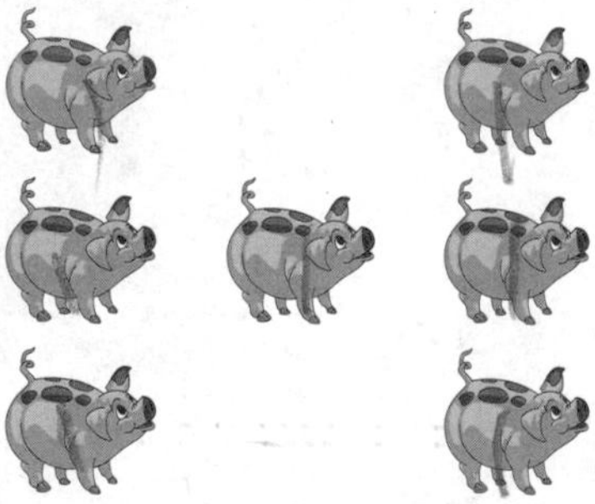

7

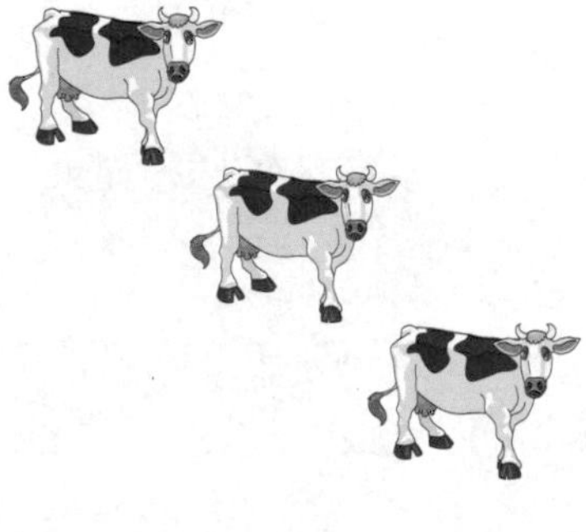

3

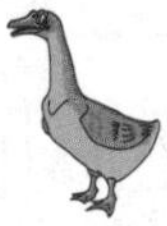

1

NAME ____________________

Lesson 1.6 Skip Counting 1 through 10

Count forward. Write a number on each  .

Count backward. Write a number on each .

Count the . Write numbers in order.

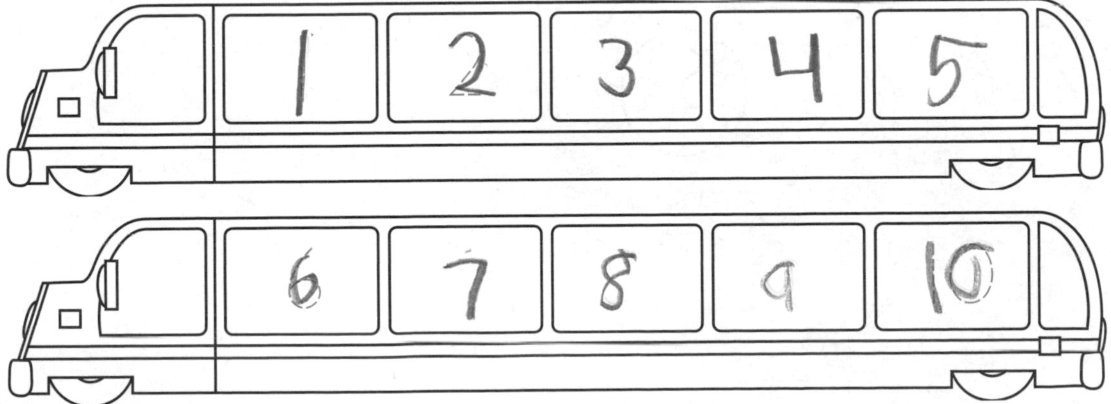

NAME ______________________________

Lesson 1.6 Skip Counting 1 through 10

Finish the pattern. Write a number in each ◯.

2 4 6 8 10

3  5 6 7

10 8  4 2

9 8 7 6 5

0  4 6 8

7 6 5 4 3

5 6 7 8 9

NAME ___________________________

Lesson 1.7 Ordinal Positions 1 through 10

Circle the fourth  from the left.

Circle the eighth  from the left.

Circle the second  from the right.

Circle the fifth  from the right.

Circle the seventh  from the right.

NAME ______________________

Lesson 1.7 Ordinal Positions 1 through 10

Circle the tenth  from the left.

Circle the first from the top.

Circle the sixth from the top.

Circle the ninth from the bottom.

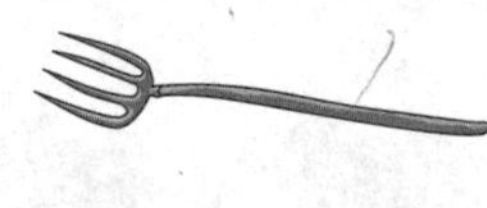
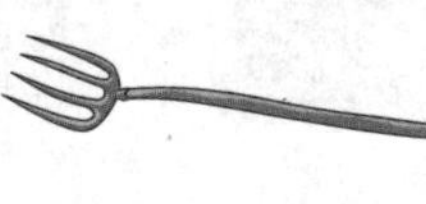
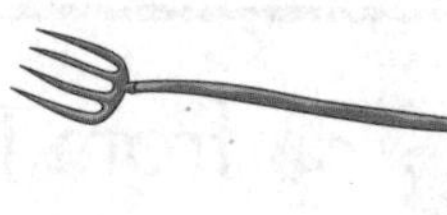

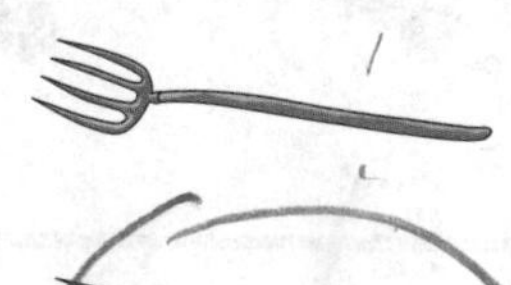
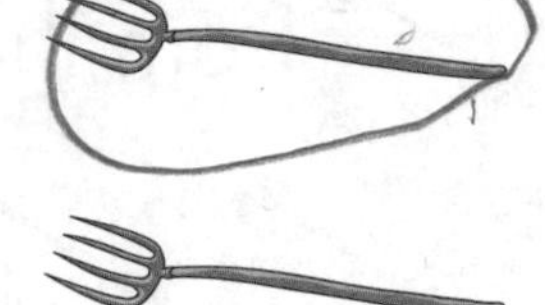

Circle the third from the bottom.

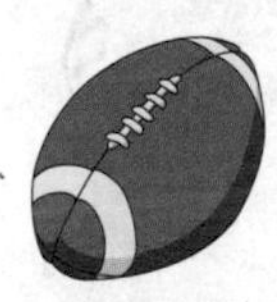

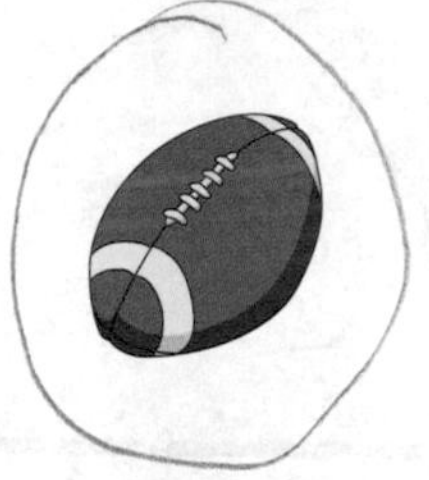

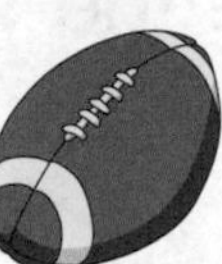

NAME ____________________

Lesson 1.8 Counting Money

1 penny	5 pennies	1 nickel

1¢	5¢	5¢

Count and write how much money.

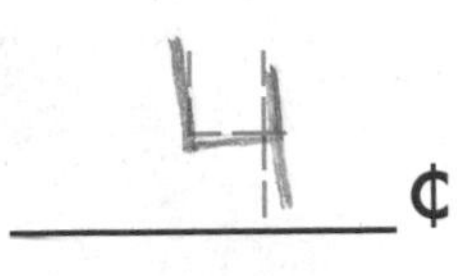
______ ¢

______ ¢

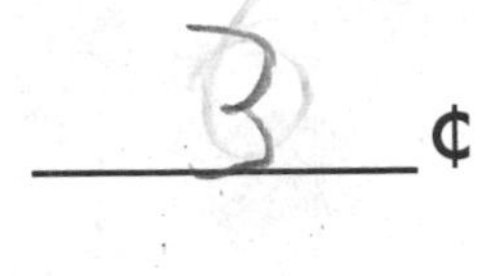
______ ¢

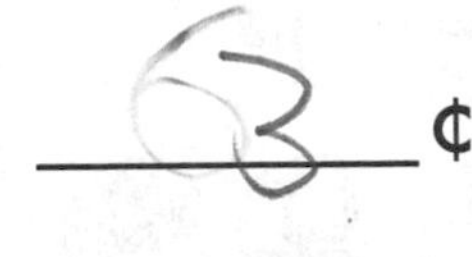
______ ¢

______ ¢

______ ¢

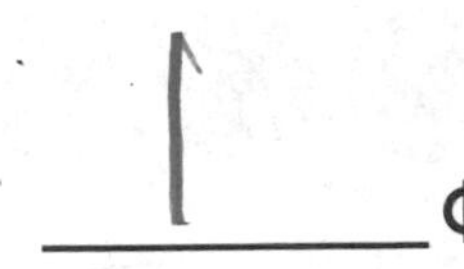
______ ¢

______ ¢

NAME ______________________

Lesson 1.8 Counting Money

1 penny

1¢

1 nickel

5¢

1 dime

10¢

Count and write how much money.

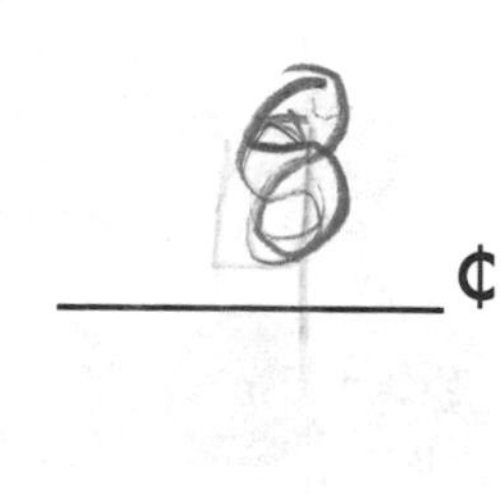

_______ ¢

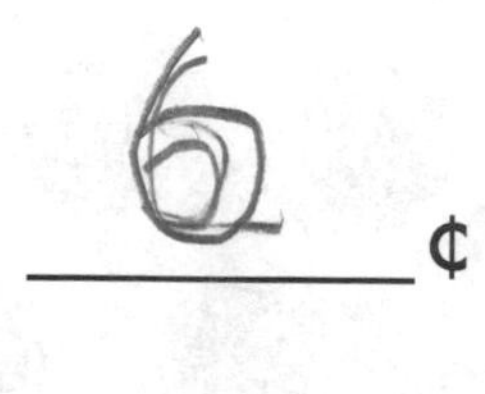

_______ ¢

_______ ¢

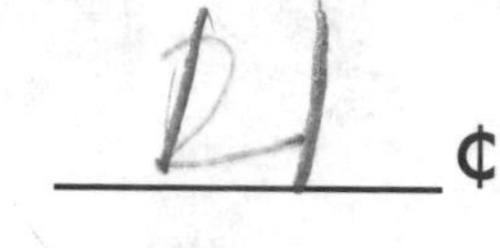

_______ ¢

_______ ¢

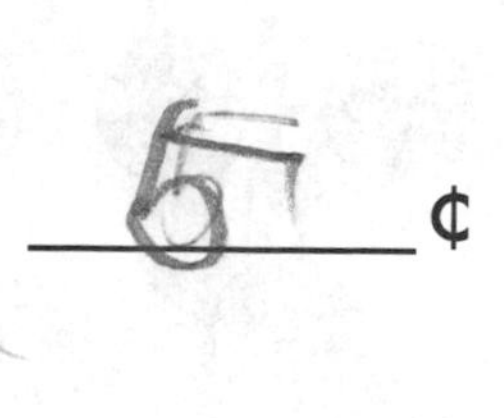

_______ ¢

_______ ¢

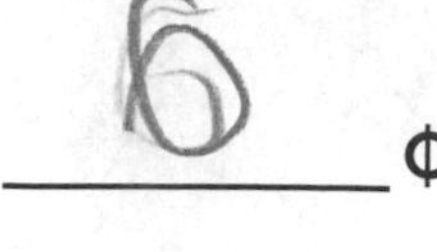

_______ ¢

NAME ____________________

Check What You Learned

Counting and Writing 0 through 10

CHAPTER 1 POSTTEST

Count how many. Write the word.

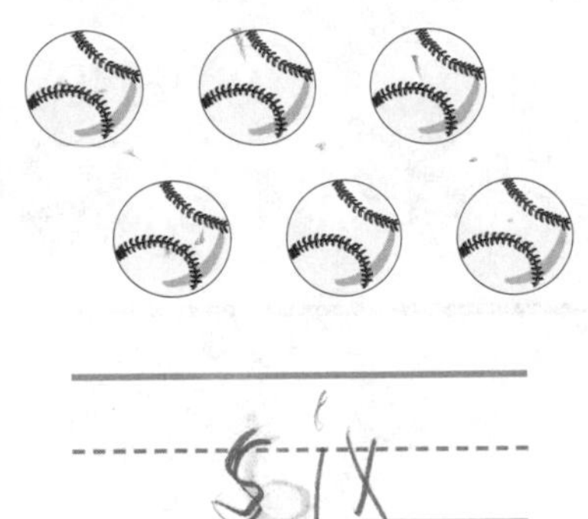

six

three

eat

Count how many. Write the number.

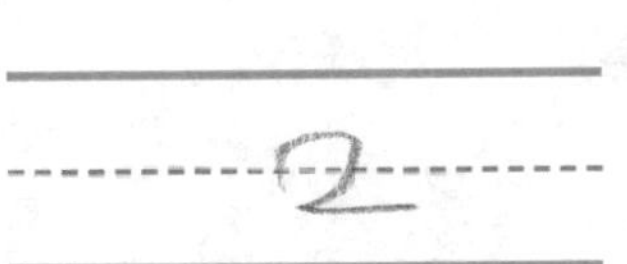

2

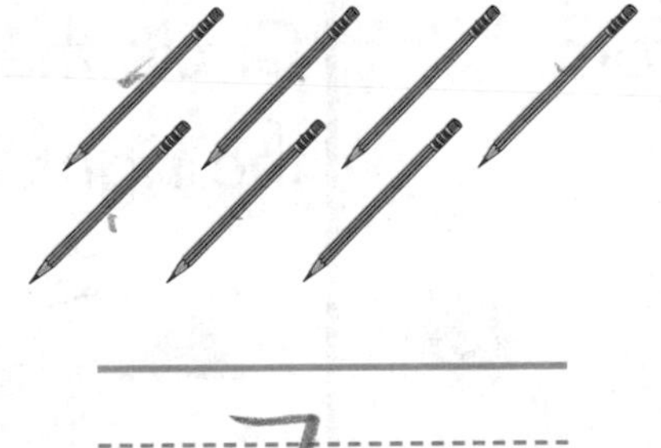

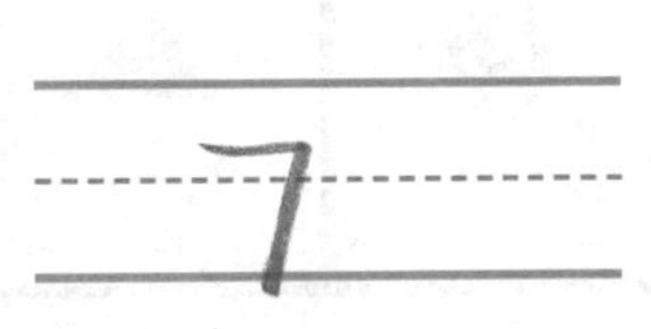

7

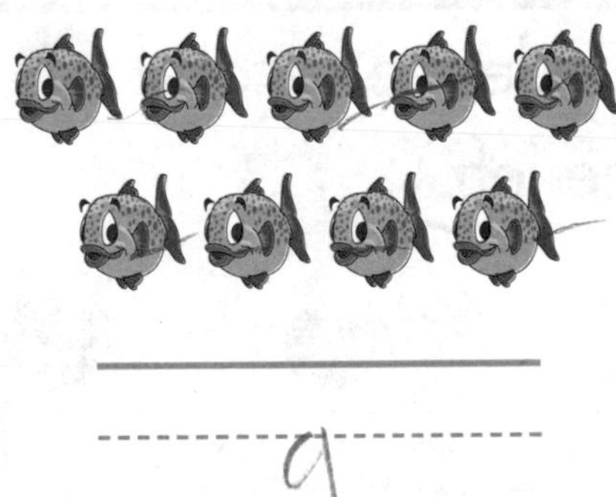

9

Finish the pattern. Write a number on each ____.

2   1   4   5   6

7   6   5   6   3

8   6   7   2   0

Check What You Learned

Counting and Writing 0 through 10

CHAPTER 1 POSTTEST

Circle the fifth  from the left.

Circle the eighth  from the right.

Circle the second ● from the left.

Circle the third ▲ from the right.

  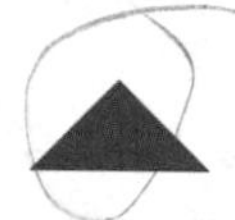 

Count and write how much money.

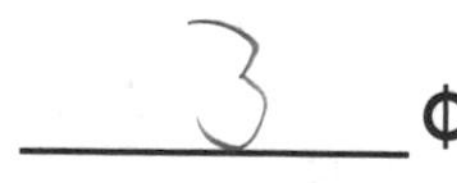 ¢

 ¢

 ¢

 ¢

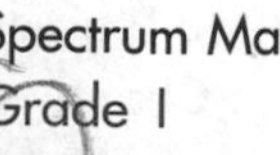

Check What You Know

Addition and Subtraction Facts through 6

Add.

5 + 1 = 6	3 + 2 = 5	1 + 1 = 2	2 + 4 = 6	6 + 0 = 6	4 + 1 = 5
4 + 0 = 4	2 + 1 = 3	3 + 0 = 3	1 + 3 = 4	4 + 2 = 6	1 + 2 = 3

0 + 6 = 6   3 + 3 = 6   0 + 4 = 4

3 + 1 = 4   2 + 4 = 6   1 + 5 = 6

Subtract.

6 − 1 = 5	4 − 2 = 2	3 − 1 = 2	5 − 3 = 2	2 − 0 = 2	4 − 1 = 3
5 − 2 = 3	6 − 4 = 2	2 − 1 = 1	3 − 2 = 1	6 − 5 = 1	5 − 0 = 5

4 − 3 = 1   6 − 2 = 4   5 − 4 = 1

6 − 3 = 3   1 − 0 = 1   2 − 2 = 0

NAME ____________________

CHAPTER 2 PRETEST

Check What You Know

SHOW YOUR WORK

Addition and Subtraction Facts through 6

Solve each problem.

There are 2 . 2 + 4 = 6

There are 4 . 

How many in all? 6

Jeff has 4 .

Karen has 1 .  4 − 1 = 3

What is the difference? 3

There are 5 .  5 − 3 = 2

3 fly away.

Subtract 5 minus 3. 2

There is 1 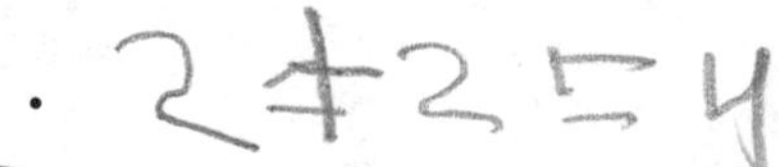. 2 + 2 = 4

There are 2 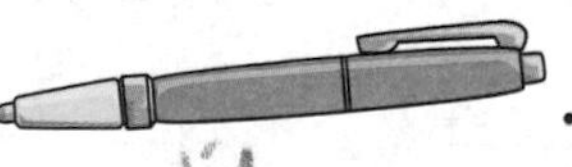.

Add 1 plus 2. 4

NAME ________________

Lesson 2.1 Adding through 3

Add.

$1 + 1 =$ 2

$\begin{array}{r} 1 \\ +1 \\ \hline 2 \end{array}$

one plus one equals two

$2 + 1 =$ 3

$\begin{array}{r} 2 \\ +1 \\ \hline 3 \end{array}$

$1 + 2 =$ 3

$\begin{array}{r} 1 \\ +2 \\ \hline 3 \end{array}$

$1 + 0 =$ 1

$\begin{array}{r} 1 \\ +0 \\ \hline 1 \end{array}$

$0 + 1 =$ 1

$\begin{array}{r} 0 \\ +1 \\ \hline 1 \end{array}$

$2 + 0 =$ 2

$\begin{array}{r} 2 \\ +0 \\ \hline 2 \end{array}$

$0 + 2 =$ 2

$\begin{array}{r} 0 \\ +2 \\ \hline 2 \end{array}$

$3 + 0 =$ 3

$\begin{array}{r} 3 \\ +0 \\ \hline 3 \end{array}$

$0 + 3 =$ 3

$\begin{array}{r} 0 \\ +3 \\ \hline 3 \end{array}$

$0 + 0 =$ 0

$\begin{array}{r} 0 \\ +0 \\ \hline 0 \end{array}$

NAME ______________________

Lesson 2.2 Subtracting from 1, 2, and 3

Subtract.

$2 - 1 =$ 1

$\begin{array}{r} 2 \\ -1 \\ \hline 1 \end{array}$

two minus one equals one

$1 - 1 =$ 0

$\begin{array}{r} 1 \\ -1 \\ \hline 0 \end{array}$

$3 - 1 =$ 2

$\begin{array}{r} 3 \\ -1 \\ \hline 2 \end{array}$

$1 - 0 =$ 1

$\begin{array}{r} 1 \\ -0 \\ \hline 1 \end{array}$

$2 - 0 =$ 2

$\begin{array}{r} 2 \\ -0 \\ \hline 2 \end{array}$

$3 - 3 =$ 0

$\begin{array}{r} 3 \\ -3 \\ \hline 0 \end{array}$

$2 - 2 =$ 0

$\begin{array}{r} 2 \\ -2 \\ \hline 0 \end{array}$

$3 - 2 =$ 1

$\begin{array}{r} 3 \\ -2 \\ \hline 1 \end{array}$

NAME ____________________

Lesson 2.3 Adding to 4 and 5

Add.

$2 + 3 =$ 5 $\begin{array}{r} 2 \\ +3 \\ \hline 5 \end{array}$

$2 + 2 =$ 4 $\begin{array}{r} 2 \\ +2 \\ \hline 4 \end{array}$

$3 + 2 =$ 5 $\begin{array}{r} 3 \\ +2 \\ \hline 5 \end{array}$

$1 + 3 =$ 4 $\begin{array}{r} 1 \\ +3 \\ \hline 4 \end{array}$

$5 + 0 =$ ______ $\begin{array}{r} 5 \\ +0 \\ \hline \end{array}$

$3 + 1 =$ 4 $\begin{array}{r} 3 \\ +1 \\ \hline 4 \end{array}$

$0 + 5 =$ ______ $\begin{array}{r} 0 \\ +5 \\ \hline \end{array}$

$0 + 4 =$ 4 $\begin{array}{r} 0 \\ +4 \\ \hline 4 \end{array}$

$4 + 1 =$ 5 $\begin{array}{r} 4 \\ +1 \\ \hline 5 \end{array}$

$4 + 0 =$ 4 $\begin{array}{r} 4 \\ +0 \\ \hline 4 \end{array}$

$1 + 4 =$ 5 $\begin{array}{r} 1 \\ +4 \\ \hline 5 \end{array}$

NAME ______________________

Lesson 2.4 Subtracting from 4 and 5

Subtract.

$5 - 2 =$ 3

$\begin{array}{r} 5 \\ -2 \\ \hline 3 \end{array}$

$4 - 4 =$ 0

$\begin{array}{r} 4 \\ -4 \\ \hline 0 \end{array}$

$4 - 2 =$ 2

$\begin{array}{r} 4 \\ -2 \\ \hline 2 \end{array}$

$5 - 1 =$ 4

$\begin{array}{r} 5 \\ -1 \\ \hline 4 \end{array}$

$5 - 0 =$ 5

$\begin{array}{r} 5 \\ -0 \\ \hline 5 \end{array}$

$4 - 1 =$ 3

$\begin{array}{r} 4 \\ -1 \\ \hline 3 \end{array}$

$4 - 3 =$ 1

$\begin{array}{r} 4 \\ -3 \\ \hline 1 \end{array}$

$5 - 4 =$ 1

$\begin{array}{r} 5 \\ -4 \\ \hline 1 \end{array}$

NAME ____________________

Lesson 2.5 Adding to 6

Add.

4 + 2 = 6

$\begin{array}{r} 4 \\ +2 \\ \hline 6 \end{array}$

5 + 1 = 6

$\begin{array}{r} 5 \\ +1 \\ \hline 6 \end{array}$

2 + 4 = 6

$\begin{array}{r} 2 \\ +4 \\ \hline 6 \end{array}$

1 + 5 = 6

$\begin{array}{r} 1 \\ +5 \\ \hline 6 \end{array}$

6 + 0 = 6

$\begin{array}{r} 6 \\ +0 \\ \hline 6 \end{array}$

3 + 3 = 6

$\begin{array}{r} 3 \\ +3 \\ \hline 6 \end{array}$

0 + 6 = 6

$\begin{array}{r} 0 \\ +6 \\ \hline 6 \end{array}$

$\begin{array}{r} 3 \\ +3 \\ \hline 6 \end{array}$ $\begin{array}{r} 4 \\ +2 \\ \hline 6 \end{array}$ $\begin{array}{r} 3 \\ +2 \\ \hline 6 \end{array}$ $\begin{array}{r} 5 \\ +1 \\ \hline 6 \end{array}$ $\begin{array}{r} 0 \\ +6 \\ \hline 6 \end{array}$ $\begin{array}{r} 1 \\ +4 \\ \hline 6 \end{array}$

2 + 3 = 6 1 + 5 = 6 3 + 3 = 6

6 + 0 = 6 2 + 4 = 6 1 + 3 = 6

NAME ____________________

Lesson 2.6 Subtracting from 6

Subtract.

$6 - 4 =$ 2

$$\begin{array}{r} 6 \\ -4 \\ \hline 2 \end{array}$$

$6 - 1 =$ 5

$$\begin{array}{r} 6 \\ -1 \\ \hline 5 \end{array}$$

$6 - 0 =$ 6

$$\begin{array}{r} 6 \\ -0 \\ \hline 6 \end{array}$$

$6 - 3 =$ 3

$$\begin{array}{r} 6 \\ -3 \\ \hline 3 \end{array}$$

$6 - 2 =$ 4

$$\begin{array}{r} 6 \\ -2 \\ \hline \end{array}$$

$6 - 5 =$ 1

$$\begin{array}{r} 6 \\ -5 \\ \hline 1 \end{array}$$

$$\begin{array}{r} 6 \\ -1 \\ \hline 5 \end{array} \quad \begin{array}{r} 6 \\ -3 \\ \hline 3 \end{array} \quad \begin{array}{r} 6 \\ -2 \\ \hline 4 \end{array} \quad \begin{array}{r} 6 \\ -6 \\ \hline 0 \end{array} \quad \begin{array}{r} 6 \\ -4 \\ \hline 2 \end{array} \quad \begin{array}{r} 6 \\ -5 \\ \hline 1 \end{array}$$

Lesson 2.7 Fact Families 0 through 6

Add or subtract.

2	3	5	5
+3	+2	−2	−3
5	5	3	2

 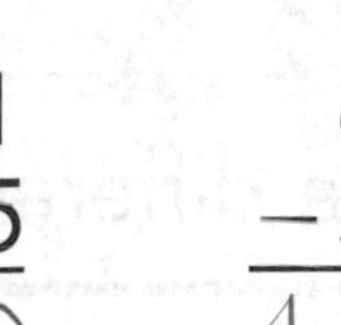

5	1	6	6
+1	+5	−5	−1
6	6	1	5

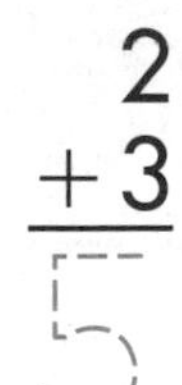   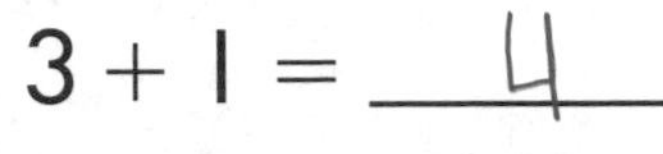  

3 + 1 = 4

1 + 3 = 4

4 − 3 = 1

4 − 1 = 3

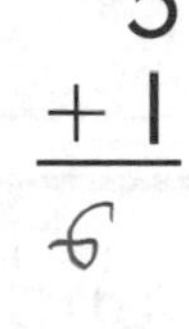  

3 + 3 = 6

6 − 3 = 2

1	2	3	3
+2	+1	−1	−2
3	3	2	1

  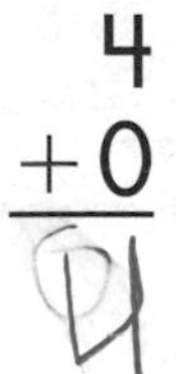 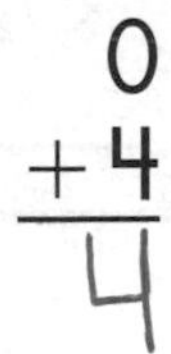 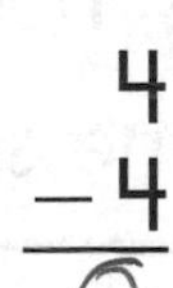

4	0	4	4
+0	+4	−4	−0
4	4	0	4

     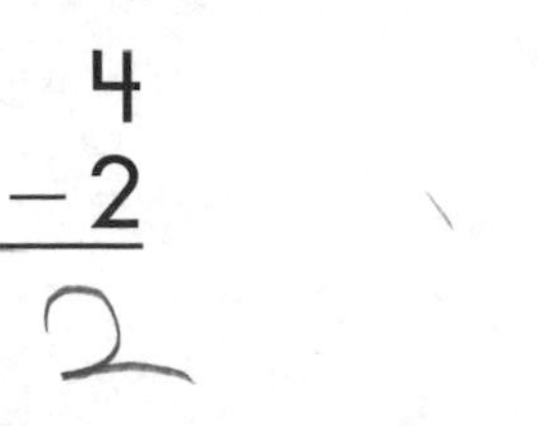

2	4
+2	−2
4	2

   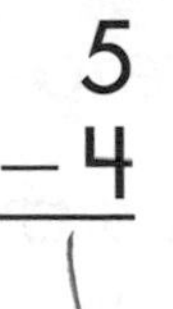 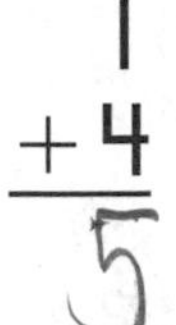

4	1	5	5
+1	+4	−4	−1
3	5	1	4

NAME ____________________

Lesson 2.8 Problem Solving

SHOW YOUR WORK

Solve each problem.

Tom has 5 .
Maria has 2 .
What is the difference? 3

$$\begin{array}{r} 5 \\ -\ 2 \\ \hline 3 \end{array}$$

There are 3 on the ground.
1 more falls to the ground.
What is 3 + 1? ________

There are 4 .
2 drive away.
How many are left? 

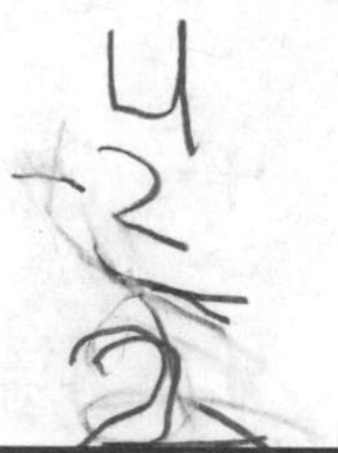

Fuji has 2 .
Steve has 1 .
What is the sum? 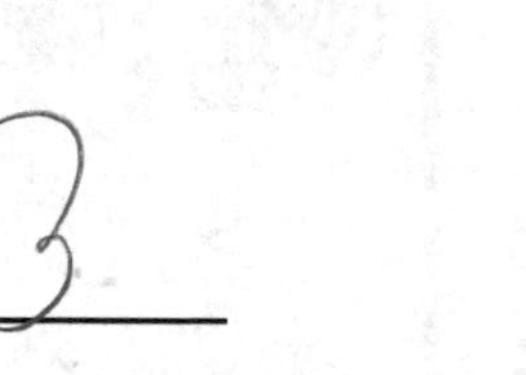

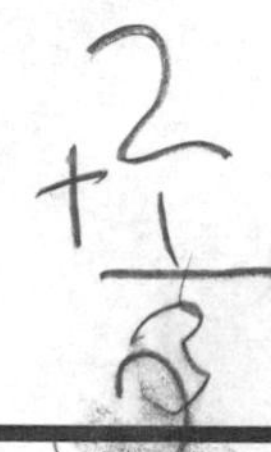

There are 2 .
Then 3 more come.
What is 2 plus 3? ________

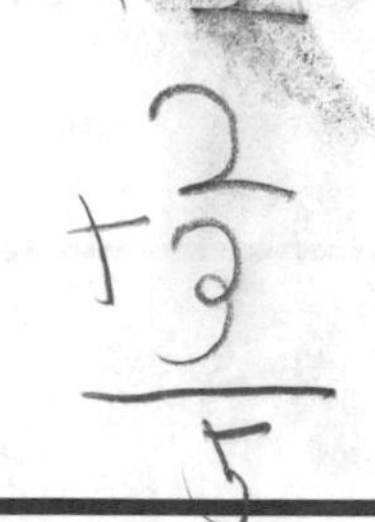

There are 6 .
1 flies away.
What is 6 minus 1? 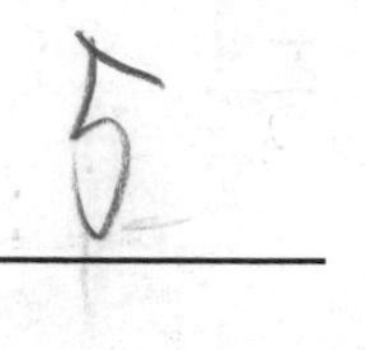

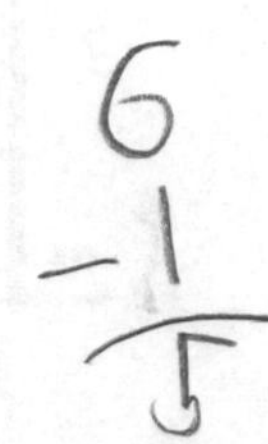

NAME ________________________

Lesson 2.8 Problem Solving

SHOW YOUR WORK

Solve each problem.

Betsy has 5 .
Drew has 1 .
Add 5 plus 1. 6

Eric saw 2 .
Esther saw 4 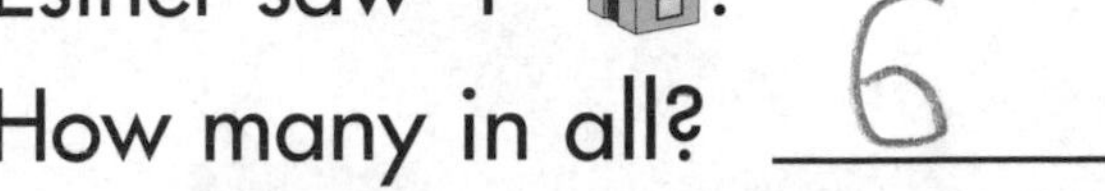.
How many in all? 6

The farmer has 3 .
The farmer gets 3 more .
How many does the farmer have? 6

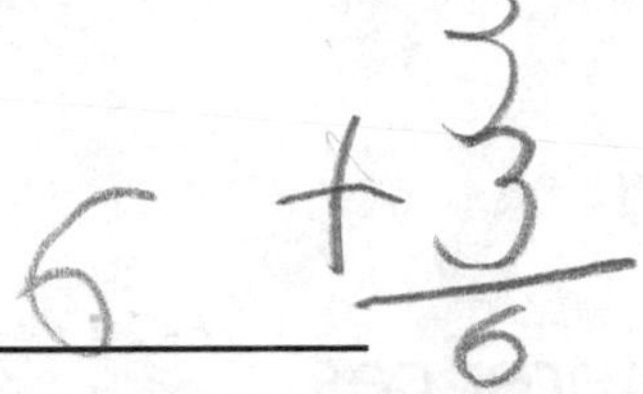

There are 3 .
I ate 1 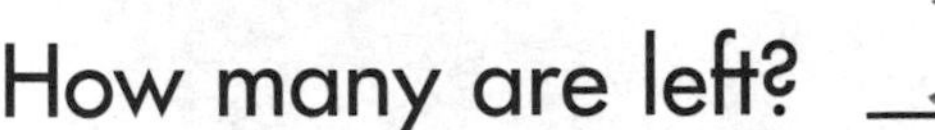.
How many are left? 2

There are 5 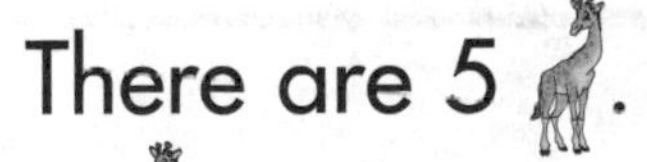.
3 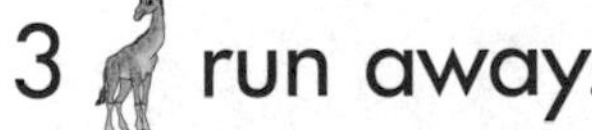 run away.
Subtract 5 − 3. 2

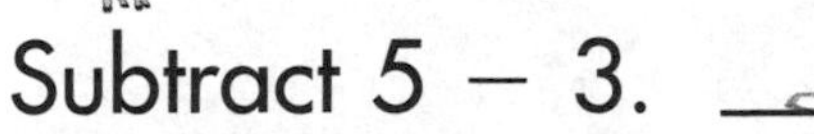

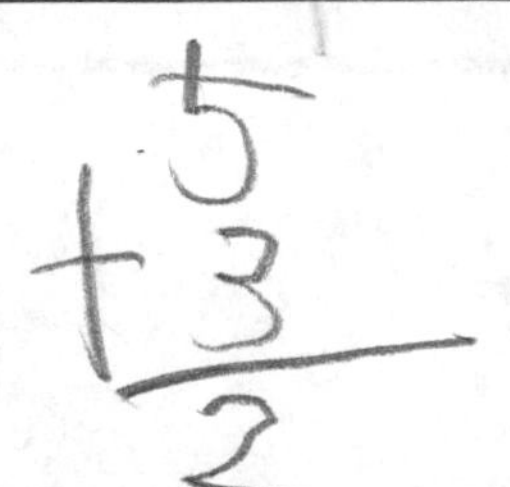

There are 6 ⚾.
I lost 2 ⚾.
How many do I have left? 4

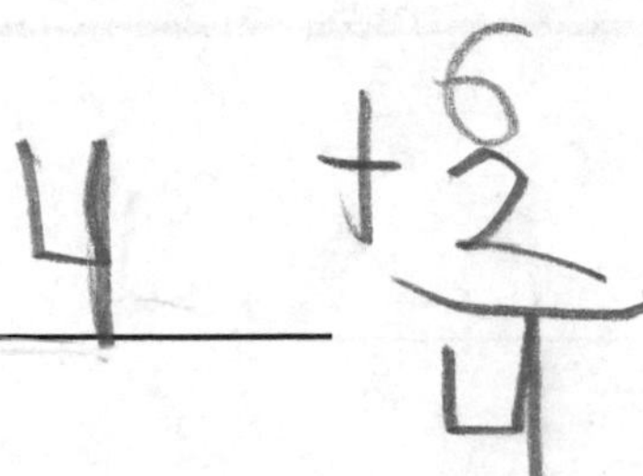

Lesson 2.8 Problem Solving

SHOW YOUR WORK

Solve each problem.

Ella has 1 .

Carlos has 1 .

What is the sum? ________

I have 1 .

I buy 4 .

What is 1 plus 4? ________

Len has 5 .

Tami has 4 .

What is the difference? ________

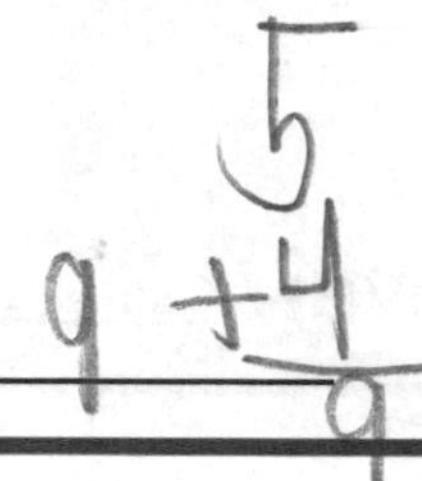

There are 4 .

3 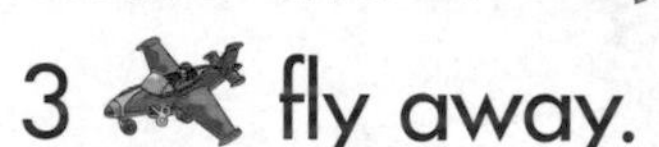 fly away.

Subtract 4 minus 3. ________

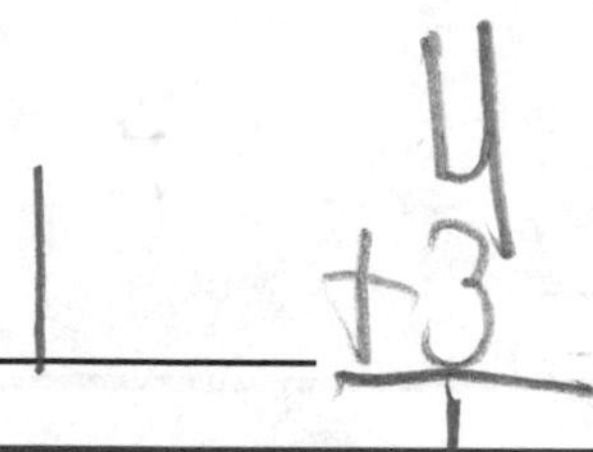

Will picked 2 .

Nita picked 2 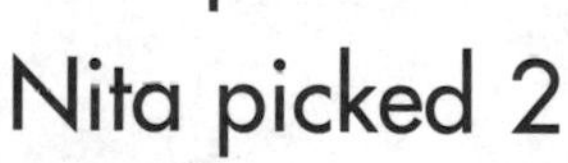.

Add 2 + 2. ________

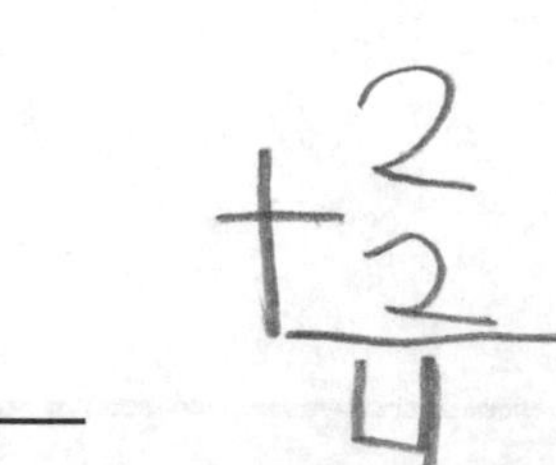

There are 6 .

I took 4 .

How many are left? ________

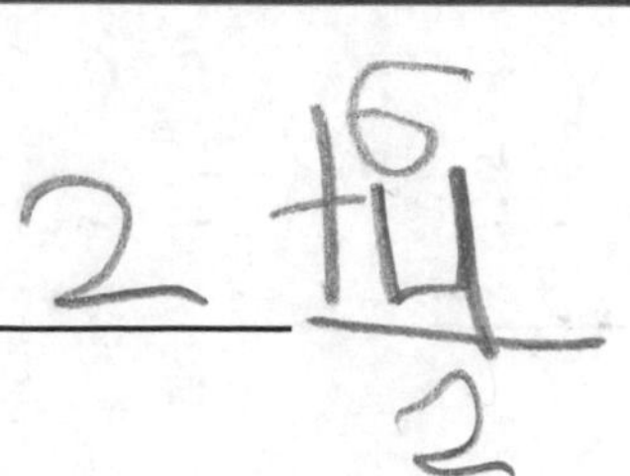

NAME ____________________

Check What You Learned

Addition and Subtraction Facts through 6

Add.

$4 + 1$	$5 + 1$	$3 + 2$	$2 + 4$	$3 + 0$	$1 + 3$
$0 + 6$	$3 + 1$	$2 + 2$	$1 + 0$	$3 + 3$	$2 + 3$
$4 + 0$	$1 + 2$	$0 + 5$	$1 + 1$	$4 + 2$	$6 + 0$

Subtract.

$3 - 0$	$6 - 1$	$4 - 4$	$5 - 2$	$3 - 2$	$6 - 0$
$6 - 4$	$5 - 3$	$2 - 0$	$6 - 3$	$5 - 5$	$4 - 3$
$4 - 1$	$5 - 4$	$6 - 2$	$2 - 1$	$5 - 1$	$6 - 6$

NAME ____________________

Check What You Learned

SHOW YOUR WORK

Addition and Subtraction Facts through 6

Solve each problem.

There are 2 .
Then 3 more  come.
Add to find the sum. 5

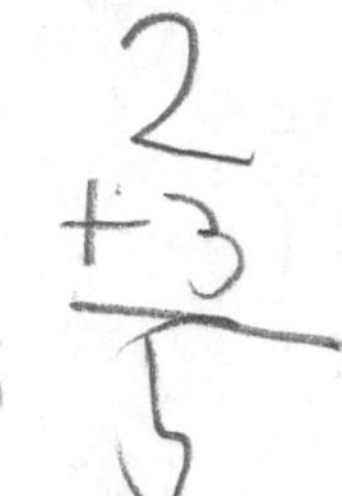

There are 5 .
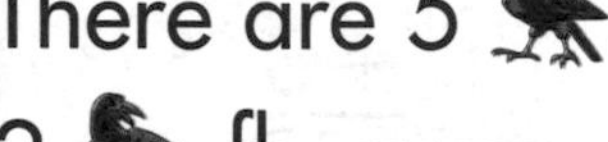 fly away.
How many are left? 3

Nate has 4 .
Jane has 1 .
What is the difference? ______

I have 3 .
I buy 3 more .
What is 3 plus 3? 6

There are 6 .
 walk away.
What is 6 minus 5? ______

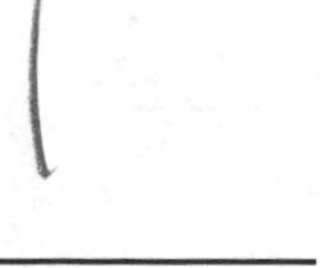

There are 3 .
Then, 1 more  comes.
How many in all? 4

NAME ______________________

Check What You Know

Addition and Subtraction Facts through 10

Add.

9 + 1	2 + 7	6 + 4	0 + 8	5 + 3	1 + 6
4 + 4	0 + 9	3 + 6	2 + 8	7 + 3	3 + 4
10 + 0	1 + 4	2 + 5	8 + 1	5 + 5	6 + 2

Subtract.

10 − 5	10 − 8	9 − 3	8 − 6	7 − 1	9 − 0
8 − 7	10 − 3	7 − 7	9 − 5	8 − 1	7 − 4
10 − 1	9 − 8	8 − 4	10 − 2	7 − 0	10 − 9

NAME ____________________

Check What You Know

SHOW YOUR WORK

Addition and Subtraction Facts through 10

Solve each problem.

There are 4 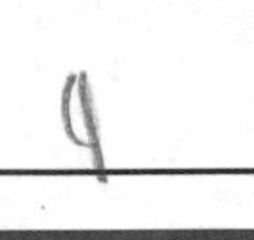.
5 more come.
Now how many are here? ________

There are 9 .
There are 6 .
How many more than are there? ________

Miguel has .
He buys  for 7¢.
How much money does he have left? ________¢

Jenny has 5 .
She finds 2 more 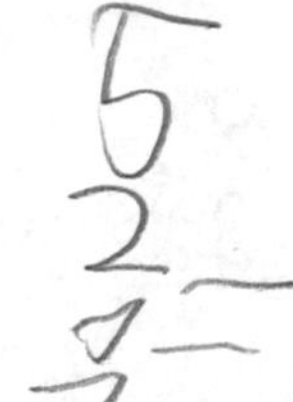.
What is the sum of 5 plus 2? ________

There are 8 .
3  ran away.
What is 8 minus 3? ________

I buy 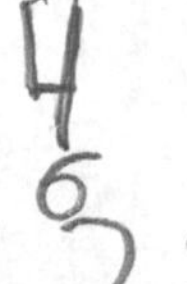 for 4¢.
I buy for 6¢.
How much money did I spend? ________¢

NAME ____________________

Lesson 3.1 Adding to 7

Add.

$5 + 2 =$ ______

$\begin{array}{r} 5 \\ +2 \\ \hline \end{array}$

$3 + 4 =$ ______

$\begin{array}{r} 3 \\ +4 \\ \hline \end{array}$

$2 + 5 =$ ______

$\begin{array}{r} 2 \\ +5 \\ \hline \end{array}$

$4 + 3 =$ ______

$\begin{array}{r} 4 \\ +3 \\ \hline \end{array}$

$6 + 1 =$ ______

$\begin{array}{r} 6 \\ +1 \\ \hline \end{array}$

$7 + 0 =$ ______

$\begin{array}{r} 7 \\ +0 \\ \hline \end{array}$

$1 + 6 =$ ______

$\begin{array}{r} 1 \\ +6 \\ \hline \end{array}$

$0 + 7 =$ ______

$\begin{array}{r} 0 \\ +7 \\ \hline \end{array}$

$\begin{array}{r} 3 \\ +4 \\ \hline \end{array}$ $\begin{array}{r} 2 \\ +5 \\ \hline \end{array}$ $\begin{array}{r} 5 \\ +1 \\ \hline \end{array}$ $\begin{array}{r} 0 \\ +7 \\ \hline \end{array}$ $\begin{array}{r} 1 \\ +6 \\ \hline \end{array}$ $\begin{array}{r} 5 \\ +2 \\ \hline \end{array}$

Lesson 3.2 Subtracting from 7

Subtract.

7 − 3 = ______

$$\begin{array}{r} 7 \\ -3 \\ \hline \end{array}$$

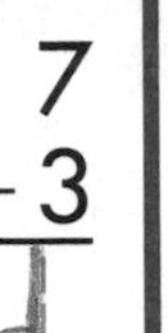

7 − 1 = ______

$$\begin{array}{r} 7 \\ -1 \\ \hline \end{array}$$

7 − 5 = ______

$$\begin{array}{r} 7 \\ -5 \\ \hline \end{array}$$

7 − 0 = ______

$$\begin{array}{r} 7 \\ -0 \\ \hline \end{array}$$

7 − 6 = ______

$$\begin{array}{r} 7 \\ -6 \\ \hline \end{array}$$

7 − 4 = ______

$$\begin{array}{r} 7 \\ -4 \\ \hline \end{array}$$

7 − 2 = ______

$$\begin{array}{r} 7 \\ -2 \\ \hline \end{array}$$

7 − 7 = ______

$$\begin{array}{r} 7 \\ -7 \\ \hline \end{array}$$

NAME ____________________

Lesson 3.3 Adding to 8

Add to find the sum.

$3 + 5 =$ ______

$\begin{array}{r} 3 \\ +5 \\ \hline \end{array}$

$2 + 6 =$ ______

$\begin{array}{r} 2 \\ +6 \\ \hline \end{array}$

$5 + 3 =$ ______

$\begin{array}{r} 5 \\ +3 \\ \hline \end{array}$

$6 + 2 =$ ______

$\begin{array}{r} 6 \\ +2 \\ \hline \end{array}$

$8 + 0 =$ ______

$\begin{array}{r} 8 \\ +0 \\ \hline \end{array}$

$4 + 4 =$ ______

$\begin{array}{r} 4 \\ +4 \\ \hline \end{array}$

$0 + 8 =$ ______

$\begin{array}{r} 0 \\ +8 \\ \hline \end{array}$

$\begin{array}{r} 4 \\ +3 \\ \hline \end{array}$ $\begin{array}{r} 2 \\ +6 \\ \hline \end{array}$ $\begin{array}{r} 1 \\ +7 \\ \hline \end{array}$ $\begin{array}{r} 8 \\ +0 \\ \hline \end{array}$ $\begin{array}{r} 6 \\ +1 \\ \hline \end{array}$ $\begin{array}{r} 5 \\ +3 \\ \hline \end{array}$

NAME ______________________

Lesson 3.4 Subtracting from 8

Subtract to find the difference.

8 − 2 = 6

$\begin{array}{r} 8 \\ -2 \\ \hline 6 \end{array}$

8 − 4 = 4

$\begin{array}{r} 8 \\ -4 \\ \hline 4 \end{array}$

8 − 6 = 2

$\begin{array}{r} 8 \\ -6 \\ \hline 2 \end{array}$

8 − 7 = 1

$\begin{array}{r} 8 \\ -7 \\ \hline 1 \end{array}$

8 − 1 = 7

$\begin{array}{r} 8 \\ -1 \\ \hline 7 \end{array}$

8 − 8 = 0

$\begin{array}{r} 8 \\ -8 \\ \hline 0 \end{array}$

8 − 3 = 5

$\begin{array}{r} 8 \\ -3 \\ \hline 5 \end{array}$

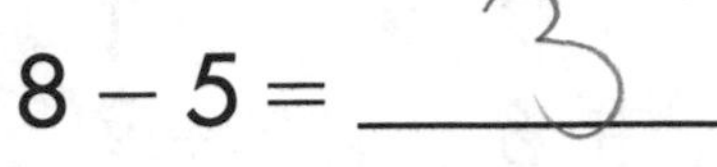

8 − 5 = 3

$\begin{array}{r} 8 \\ -5 \\ \hline 3 \end{array}$

NAME ____________________

Lesson 3.5 Adding to 9

Add to find the sum.

$3 + 6 =$ ______

$$\begin{array}{r} 3 \\ +6 \\ \hline \end{array}$$

$1 + 8 =$ ______

$$\begin{array}{r} 1 \\ +8 \\ \hline \end{array}$$

$6 + 3 =$ ______

$$\begin{array}{r} 6 \\ +3 \\ \hline \end{array}$$

$8 + 1 =$ ______

$$\begin{array}{r} 8 \\ +1 \\ \hline \end{array}$$

$9 + 0 =$ ______

$$\begin{array}{r} 9 \\ +0 \\ \hline \end{array}$$

$5 + 4 =$ ______

$$\begin{array}{r} 5 \\ +4 \\ \hline \end{array}$$

$0 + 9 =$ ______

$$\begin{array}{r} 0 \\ +9 \\ \hline \end{array}$$

$4 + 5 =$ ______

$$\begin{array}{r} 4 \\ +5 \\ \hline \end{array}$$

$2 + 7 =$ ______

$$\begin{array}{r} 2 \\ +7 \\ \hline \end{array}$$

$7 + 2 =$ ______

$$\begin{array}{r} 7 \\ +2 \\ \hline \end{array}$$

$$\begin{array}{r} 4 \\ +5 \\ \hline \end{array} \quad \begin{array}{r} 2 \\ +7 \\ \hline \end{array} \quad \begin{array}{r} 0 \\ +9 \\ \hline \end{array} \quad \begin{array}{r} 6 \\ +3 \\ \hline \end{array} \quad \begin{array}{r} 7 \\ +2 \\ \hline \end{array} \quad \begin{array}{r} 1 \\ +8 \\ \hline \end{array}$$

NAME ____________________

Lesson 3.6 Subtracting from 9

Subtract to find the difference.

$9 - 7 =$ 2

$\begin{array}{r} 9 \\ -7 \\ \hline 2 \end{array}$

$9 - 3 =$ 6

$\begin{array}{r} 9 \\ -3 \\ \hline 6 \end{array}$

$9 - 5 =$ 4

$\begin{array}{r} 9 \\ -5 \\ \hline 4 \end{array}$

$9 - 1 =$ 8

4

$\begin{array}{r} 9 \\ -1 \\ \hline 8 \end{array}$

$9 - 2 =$ 7

$\begin{array}{r} 9 \\ -2 \\ \hline 7 \end{array}$

$9 - 4 =$ 5

$\begin{array}{r} 9 \\ -4 \\ \hline 5 \end{array}$

$\begin{array}{r} 9 \\ -6 \\ \hline \end{array}$ $\quad$ $\begin{array}{r} 9 \\ -9 \\ \hline \end{array}$ $\quad$ $\begin{array}{r} 9 \\ -0 \\ \hline \end{array}$ $\quad$ $\begin{array}{r} 9 \\ -8 \\ \hline \end{array}$

NAME ____________________

Lesson 3.7 Adding to 10

Add to find the sum.

4 + 6 = 10

$\begin{array}{r} 4 \\ +6 \\ \hline 10 \end{array}$

8 + 2 = 10

$\begin{array}{r} 8 \\ +2 \\ \hline 10 \end{array}$

6 + 4 = 10

$\begin{array}{r} 6 \\ +4 \\ \hline 10 \end{array}$

2 + 8 = 10

$\begin{array}{r} 2 \\ +8 \\ \hline 10 \end{array}$

1 + 9 = 10

$\begin{array}{r} 1 \\ +9 \\ \hline 10 \end{array}$

3 + 7 = 10

$\begin{array}{r} 3 \\ +7 \\ \hline 10 \end{array}$

9 + 1 = 10

$\begin{array}{r} 9 \\ +1 \\ \hline 10 \end{array}$

7 + 3 = 10

$\begin{array}{r} 7 \\ +3 \\ \hline 10 \end{array}$

$\begin{array}{r} 4 \\ +6 \\ \hline 10 \end{array}$ $\begin{array}{r} 5 \\ +5 \\ \hline 10 \end{array}$ $\begin{array}{r} 10 \\ +0 \\ \hline 10 \end{array}$ $\begin{array}{r} 3 \\ +7 \\ \hline 10 \end{array}$ $\begin{array}{r} 8 \\ +2 \\ \hline 10 \end{array}$ $\begin{array}{r} 9 \\ +1 \\ \hline 10 \end{array}$

Lesson 3.8 Subtracting from 10

Subtract to find the difference.

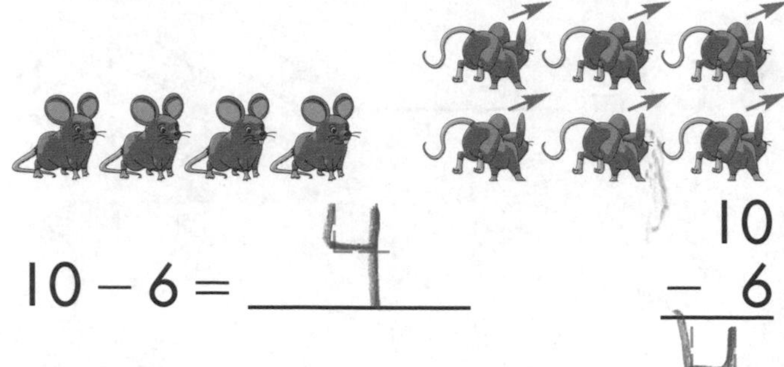

10 – 6 = ______

$\begin{array}{r} 10 \\ -\ 6 \\ \hline \end{array}$

10 – 5 = ______

$\begin{array}{r} 10 \\ -\ 5 \\ \hline \end{array}$

10 – 3 = ______

$\begin{array}{r} 10 \\ -\ 3 \\ \hline \end{array}$

10 – 8 = ______

$\begin{array}{r} 10 \\ -\ 8 \\ \hline \end{array}$

10 – 1 = ______

$\begin{array}{r} 10 \\ -\ 1 \\ \hline \end{array}$

10 – 10 = ______

$\begin{array}{r} 10 \\ -10 \\ \hline \end{array}$

10 – 2 = ______

$\begin{array}{r} 10 \\ -\ 2 \\ \hline \end{array}$

10 – 9 = ______

$\begin{array}{r} 10 \\ -\ 9 \\ \hline \end{array}$

10 – 7 = ______

$\begin{array}{r} 10 \\ -\ 7 \\ \hline \end{array}$

10 – 4 = ______

$\begin{array}{r} 10 \\ -\ 4 \\ \hline \end{array}$

NAME ______________________

Lesson 3.9 Addition Practice through 10

Add.

3 + 5	1 + 8	7 + 2	4 + 6	4 + 4	2 + 5
4 + 5	3 + 4	9 + 1	0 + 10	6 + 3	3 + 7
8 + 0	3 + 7	0 + 7	6 + 2	7 + 3	0 + 9
6 + 1	5 + 2	8 + 2	5 + 5	4 + 3	2 + 7
9 + 0	6 + 4	1 + 6	3 + 0	2 + 8	5 + 3
5 + 4	2 + 4	7 + 0	8 + 1	10 + 0	1 + 2

NAME ______________________

Lesson 3.9 Problem Solving

SHOW YOUR WORK

Solve each problem.

There are 8 .
There are 2 .
What is the sum? ______

There are 6 .
3 more come.
What is 6 plus 3? ______

I have 4 .
I buy 4 more .
How many do I have now? ______

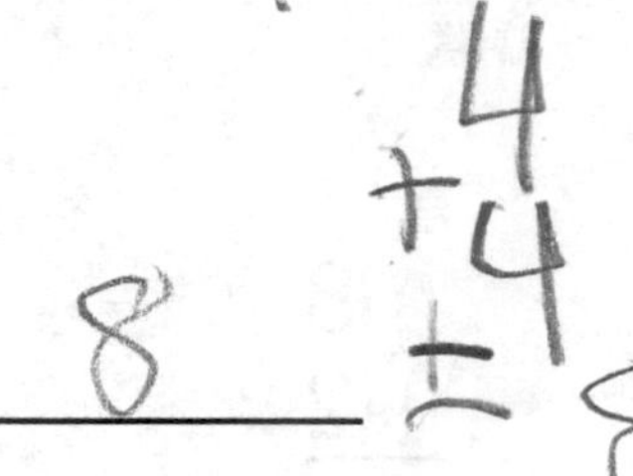

Ivan has 2 .
Helen has 5 .
What is 2 + 5? ______

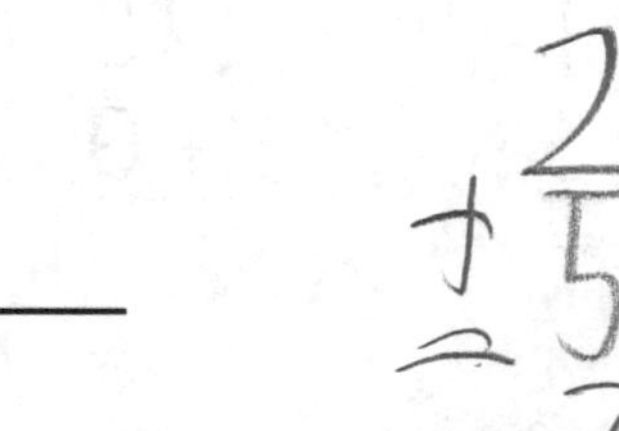

There are 7 .
3 more come.
How many in all? ______

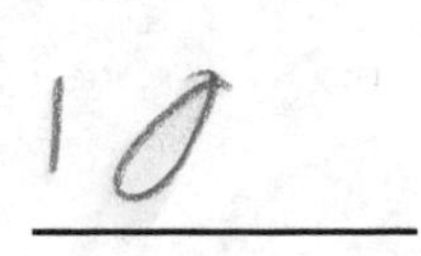

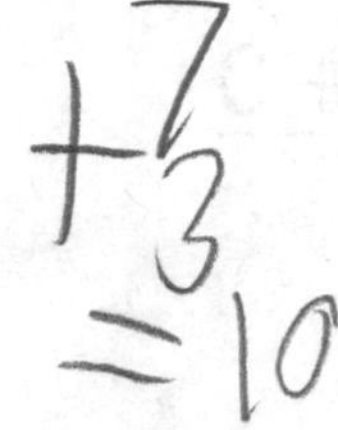

NAME ____________________

Lesson 3.10 Subtraction Practice through 10

Subtract.

10 − 4	9 − 8	9 − 3	9 − 5	10 − 1	7 − 7
7 − 5	8 − 0	9 − 5	9 − 6	7 − 3	10 − 10
10 − 7	8 − 8	10 − 5	6 − 3	9 − 1	7 − 0
8 − 3	10 − 9	9 − 9	8 − 2	5 − 1	10 − 0
9 − 4	7 − 6	8 − 1	10 − 3	9 − 0	4 − 2
10 − 8	8 − 6	4 − 1	9 − 2	10 − 6	7 − 4

NAME ____________________

Lesson 3.10 Problem Solving

SHOW YOUR WORK

Solve each problem.

There are 7 fish.
4 fish swim away.
How many are left? ______

Brian wants 10 cars.
He has 3 cars.
What is the difference? ______

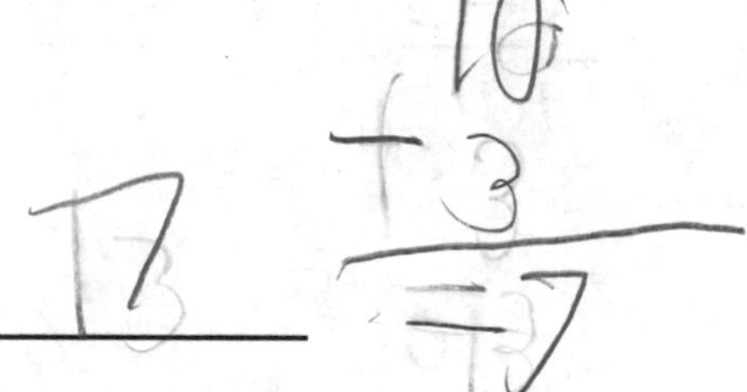

Marla has 8 bananas.
She gives 4 bananas away.
What is 8 minus 4? ______

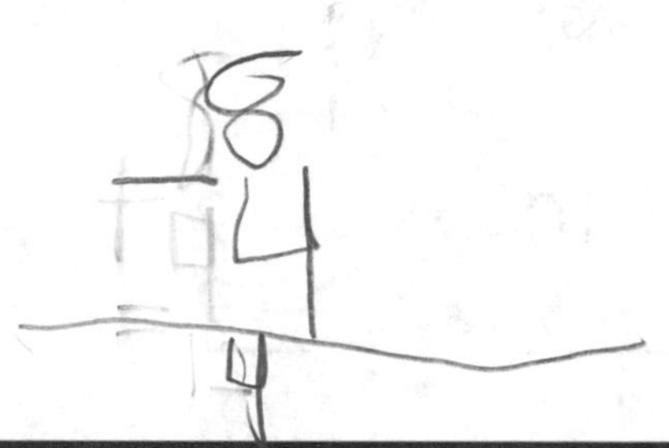

There are 7 balloons.
2 balloons pop.
How many are left? ______

Joan has 9 pencils.
Diego has 5 pencils.
What is the difference? ______

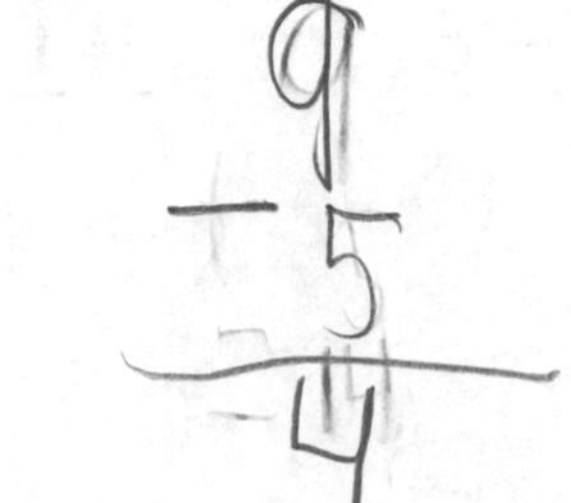

Lesson 3.11 Money

1 penny	1 nickel	1 dime

1¢	5¢	10¢

Count and write how much money.

   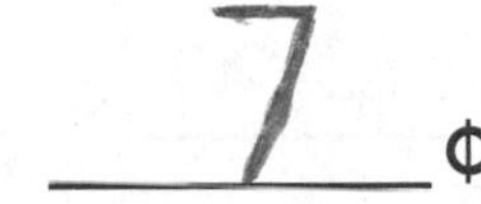 ______¢	 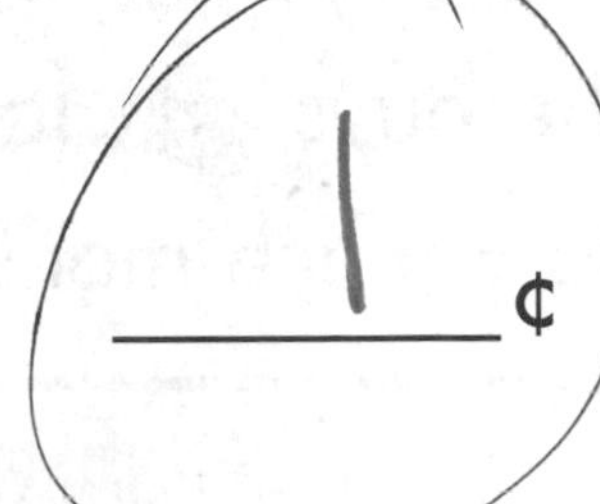 ______¢
  ______¢	 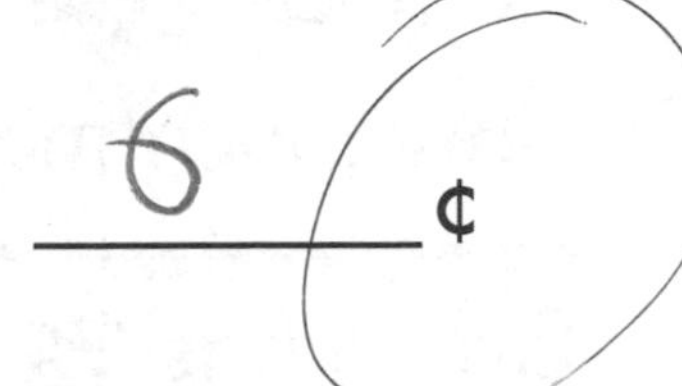 ______¢
 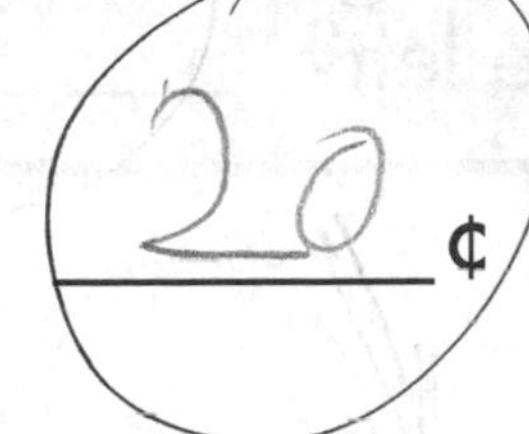 ______¢	 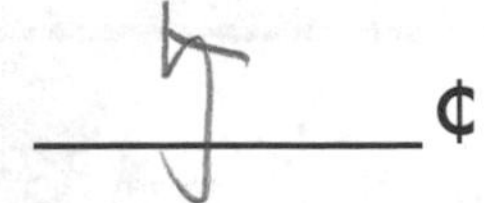 ______¢
 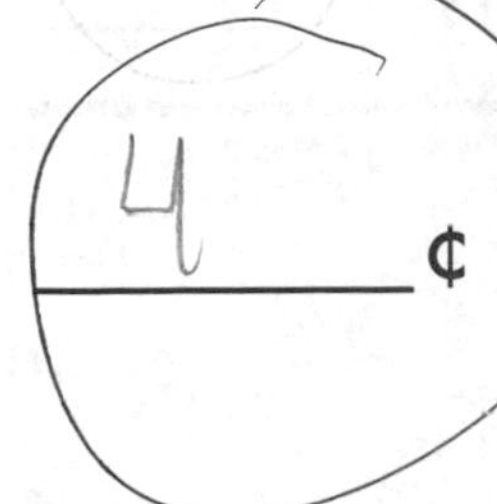 ______¢	  ______¢

NAME ______________________

Lesson 3.12 Problem Solving

SHOW YOUR WORK

Solve each problem.

John has .
He buys 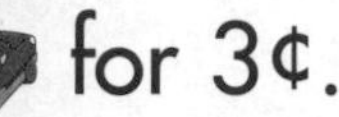 for 3¢.
How much money does he have left? ________¢

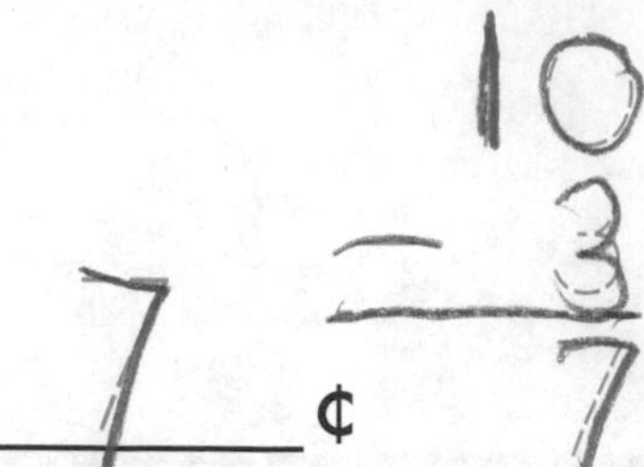

Ines buys  for 6¢.
She buys  for 4¢.
How much money did she spend? ________¢

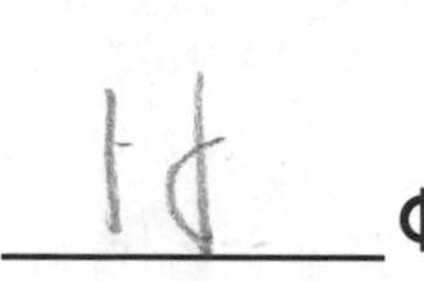

Jordan has .
He finds .
How much money does he have? ________¢

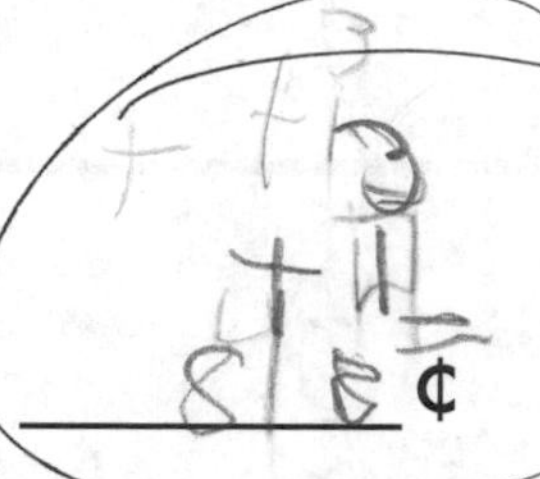

Elaine has 9¢.
She gives  to Maxine.
How much money does Elaine have left? ________¢

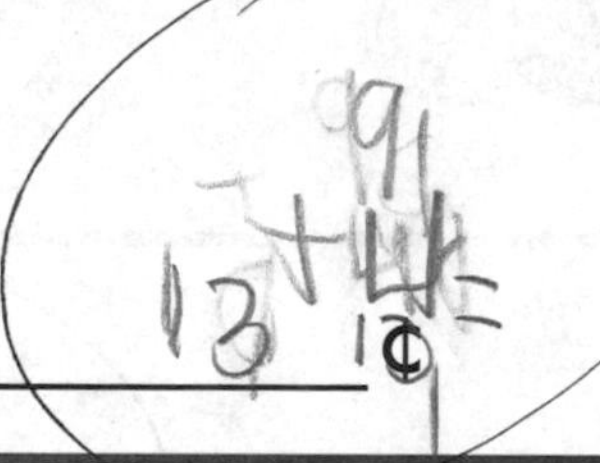

Victor has .
He buys a pencil for 6¢.
How much money does he have left? ________¢

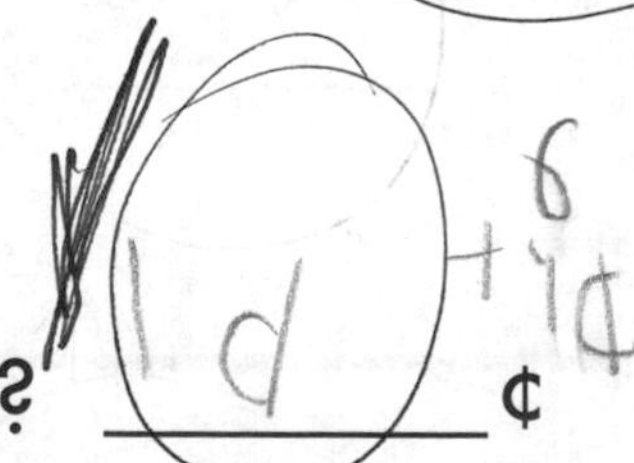

Lin buys  for 5¢.
Barb buys  for 4¢.
How much money did they spend? ________¢

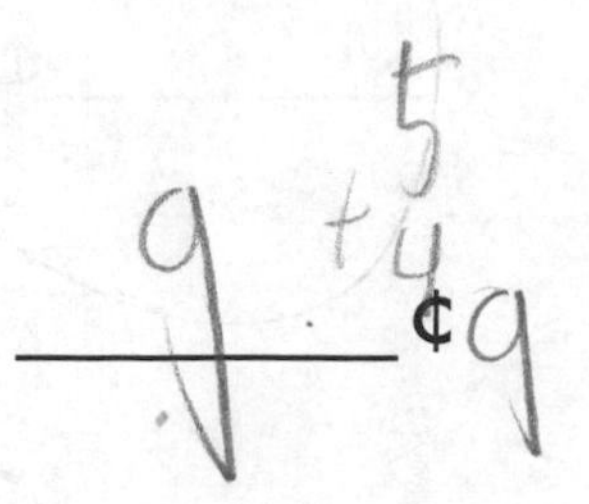

NAME ____________________

Lesson 3.13 Fact Families 7 through 10

Add or subtract.

4	5	9	9
+5	+4	−4	−5

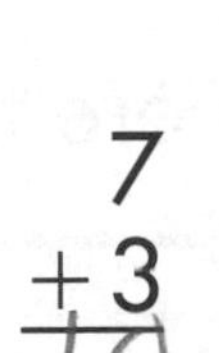

3	7	10	10
+7	+3	− 3	− 7

5 + 2 = ______

2 + 5 = ______

7 − 5 = ______

7 − 2 = ______

6 + 3 = ______

3 + 6 = ______

9 − 6 = ______

9 − 3 = ______

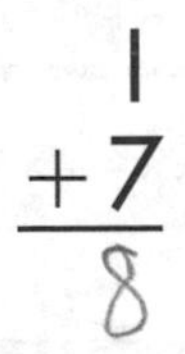

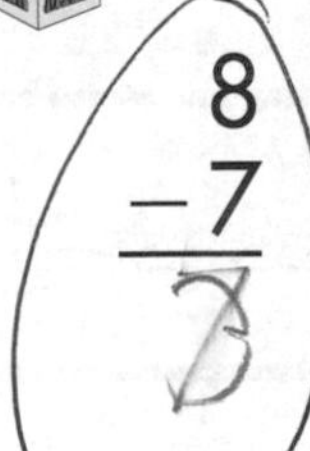

1	7	8	8
+7	+1	−1	−7

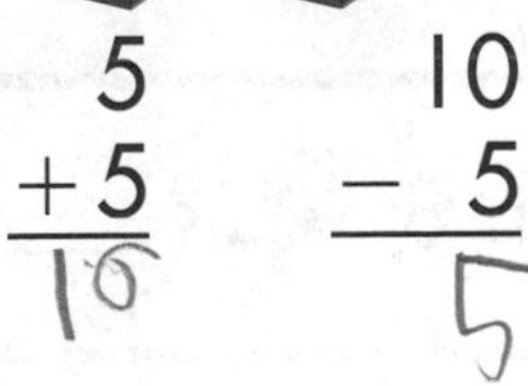

5	10
+5	− 5

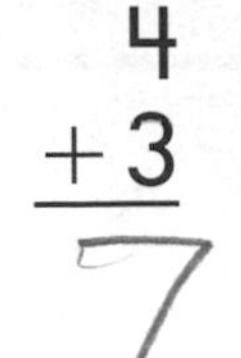
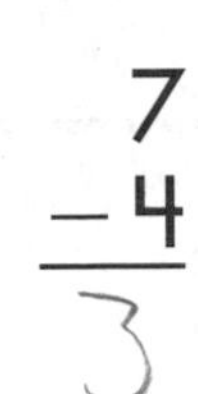
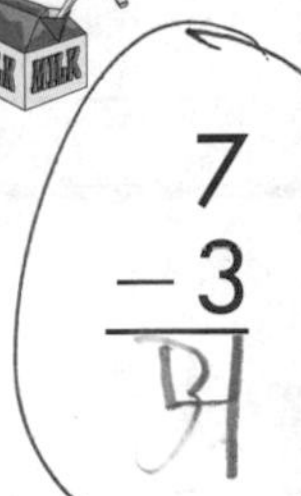

4	3	7	7
+3	+4	−4	−3

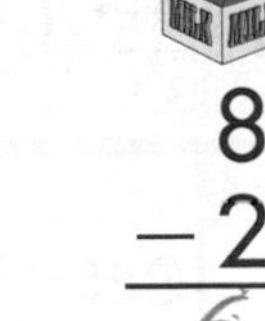
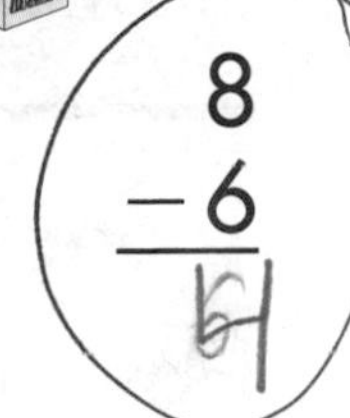

2	6	8	8
+6	+2	−2	−6

NAME ______________________

Lesson 3.14 More- and Less-Than Facts through 10

SHOW YOUR WORK

Add to find more than. Subtract to find less than.

How many is 2 more than 7  ? 9 2 + 7 = 9

What is 1 more than 8  ? 9  1+8=9

There are 2 less than 10 fish.
How many  are there? 9 2+10=9

What is 1 less than 9  ? 8 1+9=8

There is 1 more than 7 giraffe.
How many  are there? 8 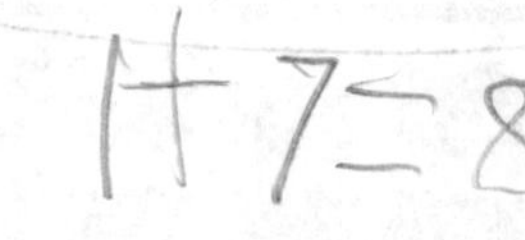 1+7=8

What is 2 less than 8  ? 6 2+8=6

How many is 1 less than 10  ? 9 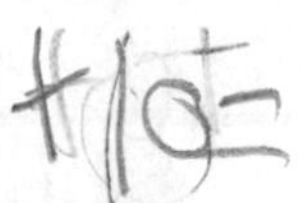

How many is 1 more than 9  ? 10 1+9=10

There is 1 less than 8 goat.
How many 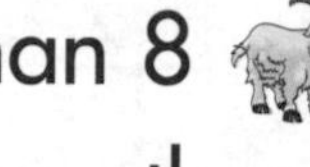 are there? 7  1+8=7

NAME ______________________

Lesson 3.15 Using Addition for Subtraction

Think addition for subtraction. Solve each problem.

8 − 4 = __4__ 4 + __12__ = 8

10 − 3 = __7__ 3 + __13__ = 10

7 − 2 = __5__ 2 + __9__ = 7

10 − 4 = __6__ 4 + __14__ = 10

5 − 1 = __4__ 1 + __6__ = 5

8 − 2 = __6__ 2 + __18__ = 8

9 − 7 = __2__ 7 + __15__ = 9

7 − 6 = __1__ 6 + __12__ = 7

8 − 5 = __3__ 5 + __12__ = 8

NAME ____________________

Lesson 3.16 Doubles and Near-Doubles

Add to find the sum.

$$\begin{array}{r} 2 \\ +2 \\ \hline \end{array}$$

$3 + 3 =$ ______ $+ 1 =$ ______

$1 + 1 =$ ______ $+ 1 =$ ______

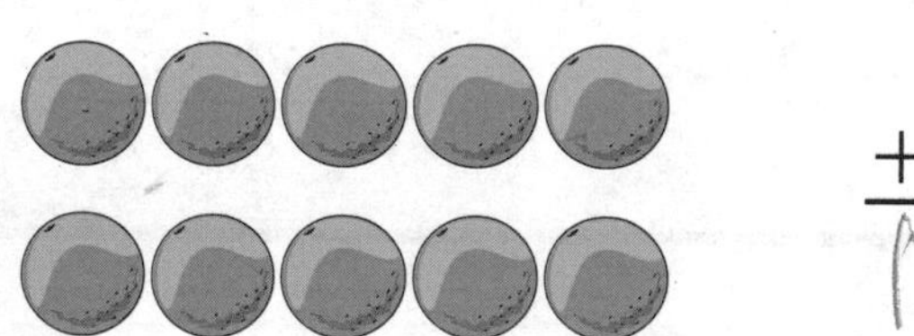

$$\begin{array}{r} 5 \\ +5 \\ \hline \end{array}$$

$$\begin{array}{r} 3 \\ +3 \\ \hline \end{array}$$

$4 + 4 =$ ______ $+ 1 =$ ______

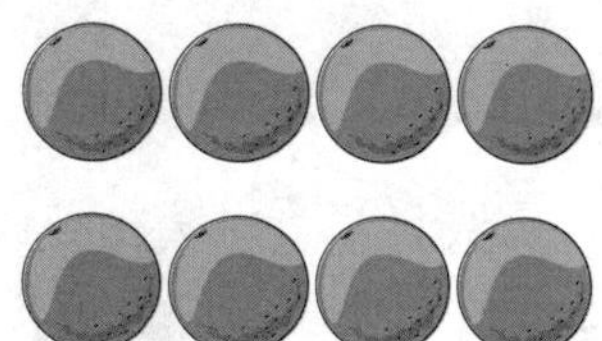

$$\begin{array}{r} 4 \\ +4 \\ \hline \end{array}$$

$$\begin{array}{r} 1 \\ +1 \\ \hline \end{array}$$

$2 + 2 =$ ______ $+ 1 =$ ______

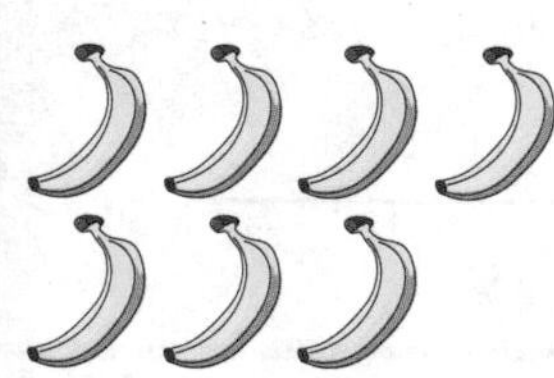

$3 + 3 =$ ______ $+ 1 =$ ______

NAME ____________________

Check What You Learned

Addition and Subtraction Facts through 10

Add.

4 + 5	0 + 7	2 + 6	8 + 2	5 + 5	1 + 8
7 + 2	1 + 9	3 + 5	6 + 1	8 + 0	3 + 7
6 + 3	4 + 4	5 + 2	10 + 0	7 + 1	4 + 3

Subtract.

9 − 7	10 − 0	10 − 6	7 − 3	8 − 8	9 − 6
10 − 2	9 − 1	9 − 4	8 − 5	8 − 3	7 − 2
7 − 6	9 − 9	10 − 7	8 − 0	10 − 4	9 − 2

NAME ______________________

Check What You Learned

SHOW YOUR WORK

Addition and Subtraction Facts through 10

Solve each problem.

There are 8 .
There are 2 .
How many more  than  are there? ________

Dan buys  for 7¢.
He buys  for 3¢.
How much money did he spend? ________¢

There are 9 .
Rachel eats 1 .
How many are left? ________

There are 4 .
3 more  come.
What is the sum? ________

Celia has .
She buys  for 8¢.
How much money does she have left? ________¢

Bob has .
He finds more.
How much money does he have? ________¢

CHAPTER 3 POSTTEST

NAME ____________________

Check What You Know

Counting and Writing through 99

Complete.

  ____ tens ____ ones = ____

  ____ tens ____ ones = ____

  ____ tens ____ one = ____

  ____ ten ____ ones = ____

Complete.

9 tens 6 ones = ____

8 tens 4 ones = ____

6 tens 3 ones = ____

5 tens 7 ones = ____

2 tens 0 ones = ____

7 tens 8 ones = ____

4 tens 9 ones = ____

1 ten 6 ones = ____

3 tens 4 ones = ____

8 tens 1 one = ____

NAME ______________________

Check What You Know

Counting and Writing through 99

Count forward or backward. Write the missing numbers.

23, 24, ____, 26, 27, ____, 29, ____, ____, 32, 33, 34

34, ____, 38, 40, 42, ____, ____, 48, 50, ____, 54, 56

88, 86, ____, 82, 80, 78, ____, 74, 72, ____, ____, 66

10, 15, ____, 25, 30, 35, ____, ____, 50, 55, ____, 65

80, ____, 70, 65, ____, 55, ____, 45, 40, ____, 30, 25

10, 20, ____, 40, ____, ____, 70, 80, ____

10 leaves

Pick a number that tells **about** how many. Circle the number.

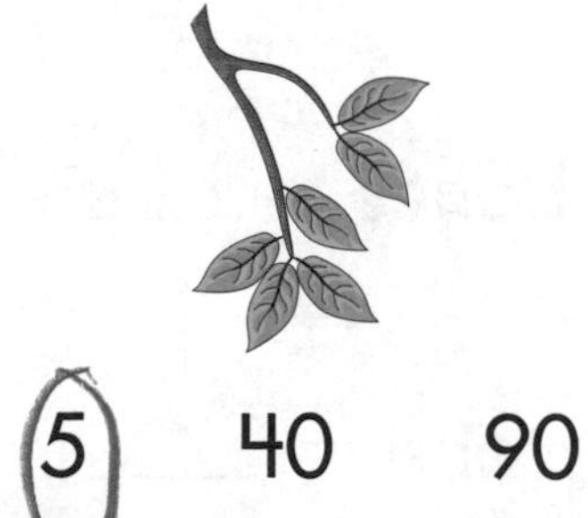

5 40 90

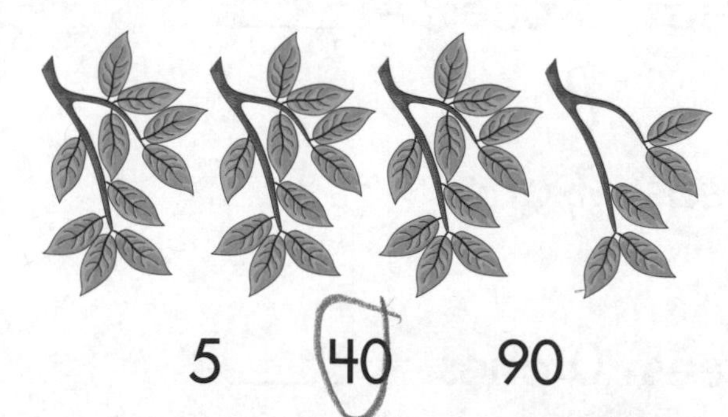

5 40 90

NAME ____________________

Lesson 4.1 Counting and Writing 10 through 14

Complete.

1 ten 0 ones = 10

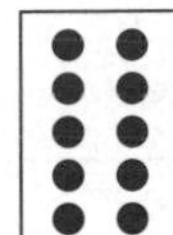

1 ten 0 ones = 10

1 ten 1 one = 11

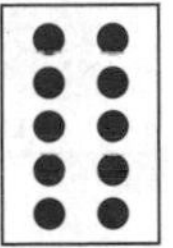 

___ ten ___ one = ___

___ ten ___ ones = ___

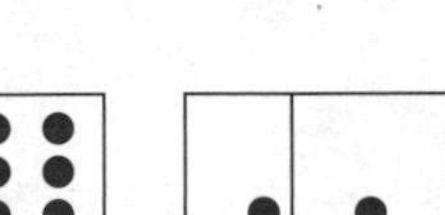

___ ten ___ ones = ___

___ ten ___ ones = ___

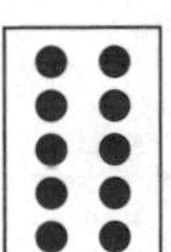 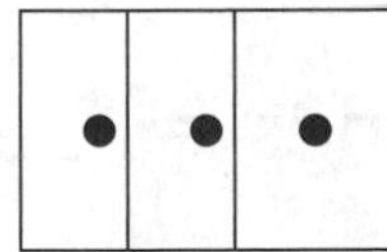

___ ten ___ ones = ___

___ ten ___ ones = ___

 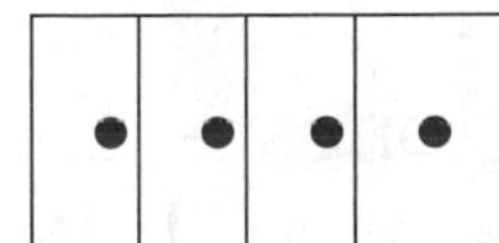

___ ten ___ ones = ___

NAME ______________________

Lesson 4.2 Counting and Writing 15 through 19

Complete.

1 ten 5 ones = 15

 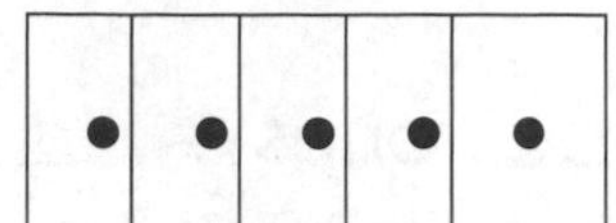

1 ten 5 ones = 15

____ ten ____ ones = ______

____ ten ____ ones = ______

____ ten ____ ones = ______

____ ten ____ ones = ______

____ ten ____ ones = ______

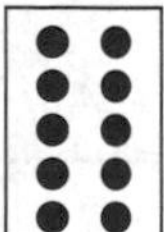

____ ten ____ ones = ______

____ ten ____ ones = ______

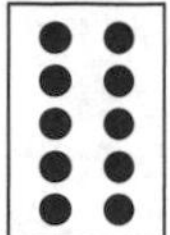 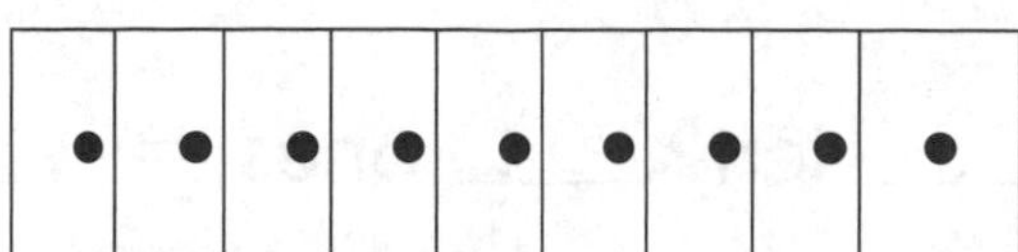

____ ten ____ ones = ______

NAME ______________________

Lesson 4.7 Counting and Writing 70 through 99

Complete.

7 tens 6 ones = 76

9 tens 8 ones = 98

8 tens 3 ones = 83

7 tens 1 one = ______

8 tens 7 ones = ______

9 tens 4 ones = ______

9 tens 2 ones = ______

7 tens 9 ones = ______

8 tens 8 ones = ______

8 tens 0 ones = ______

7 tens 5 ones = ______

9 tens 9 ones = ______

9 tens 1 one = ______

8 tens 6 ones = ______

7 tens 0 ones = ______

8 tens 2 ones = ______

NAME ____________________

Lesson 4.8 Skip Counting

Count forward. Write the missing numbers.

36, 37, 38, 39, 40, 41, 42, 43, 44, 45, 46

42, 44, ____, 48, 50, ____, 54, 56, ____, ____, 62, 64

____, 28, 30, ____, 34, 36, ____, 40, 42, 44, ____, 48

20, 25, ____, 35, 40, ____, 50, ____, 60, 65, ____, 75

____, 10, 15, ____, 25, 30, 35, ____, 45, 50, 55, ____

____, 20, 30, ____, 50, ____, 70, 80, ____

Count backward. Write the missing numbers.

79, ____, 77, 76, ____, 74, 73, 72, ____, 70, 69, ____

84, ____, 80, 78, ____, 74, 72, 70, ____, ____, 64, 62

24, 22, ____, 18, 16, ____, 12, ____, 8, 6, ____, 2

95, ____, 85, 80, ____, 70, 65, ____, ____, 50, 45, 40

75, 70, ____, 60, 55, ____, 45, 40, 35, ____, 25, ____

90, ____, 70, 60, ____, ____, 30, ____, 10

NAME ______________________________

Lesson 4.9 Estimating

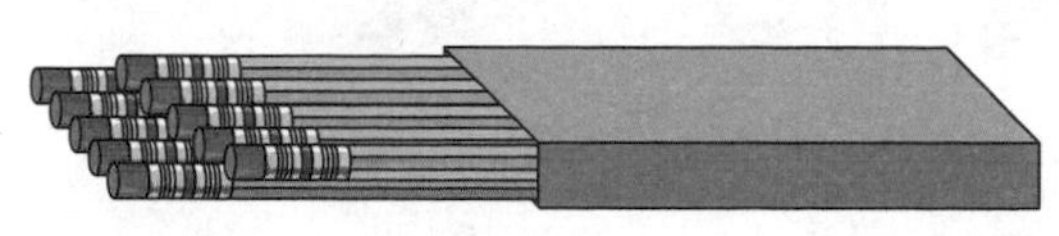

10 pencils

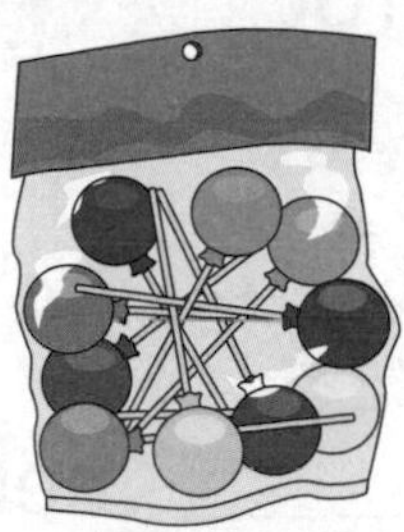

10 candies

Pick a number that tells **about** how many. Circle the number.

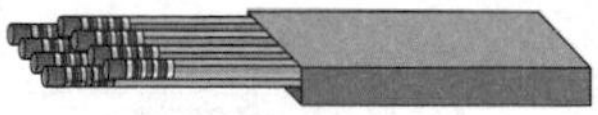

5 40 90	5 40 90
5 40 90	5 40 90
5 40 90	5 40 90

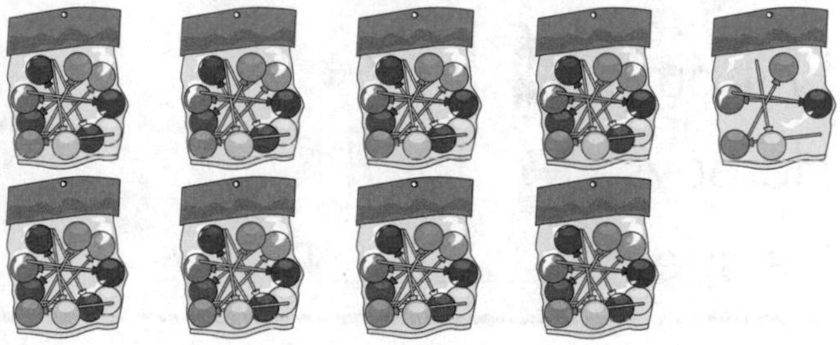

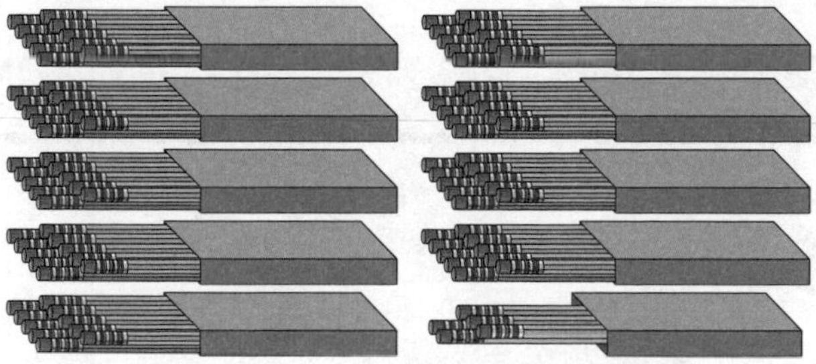

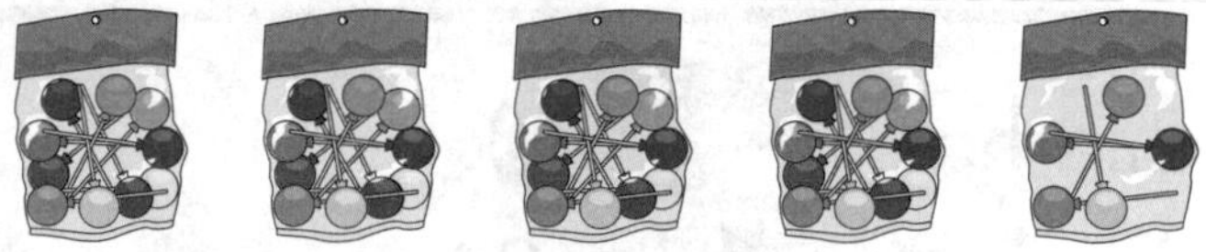

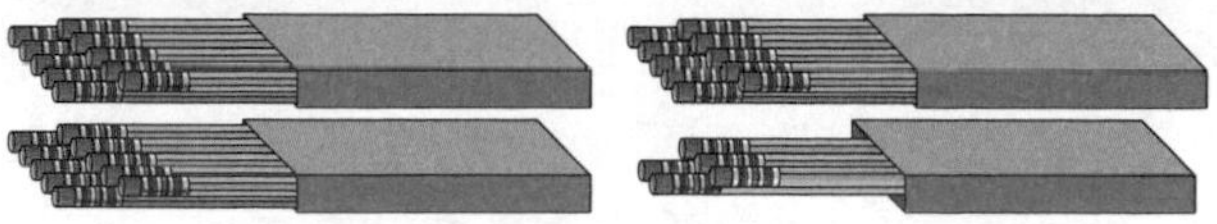

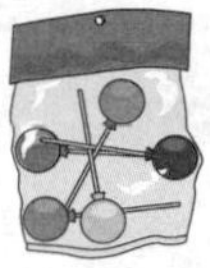

NAME ____________________

Lesson 4.10 Problem Solving

SHOW YOUR WORK

Add or subtract.

David has .
He buys  for 7¢.
He has ___3___ ¢ left.

$$\begin{array}{r} 10¢ \\ -\ 7¢ \\ \hline 3¢ \end{array}$$

Mary buys  for .
She buys  for .
She spent ________ ¢.

Phil buys  for 6¢.
He buys  for 4¢.
He spent ________ ¢.

Crystal has .
Saul has .
They have ________ ¢.

Rita has .
She buys  for 8¢.
She has ________ ¢ left.

Bob has .
Renee has .
They have ________ ¢.

Check What You Learned

Counting and Writing through 99

Complete.

____ tens ____ ones = ______

____ tens ____ ones = ______

____ tens ____ ones = ______

____ ten ____ ones = ______

4 tens 8 ones = ______

7 tens 3 ones = ______

9 tens 5 ones = ______

6 tens 2 ones = ______

5 tens 6 ones = ______

8 tens 1 one = ______

5 tens 8 ones = ______

3 tens 9 ones = ______

2 tens 7 ones = ______

1 ten 1 one = ______

NAME ______________________

Check What You Learned

Counting and Writing through 99

Count forward or backward. Write the missing numbers.

47, 48, ____, 50, 51, ____, ____, 54, 55, ____, 57, 58

____, 26, 28, ____, 32, 34, 36, ____, ____, 42, 44, 46

68, ____, 64, 62, ____, 58, 56, ____, 52, 50, ____, 46

____, 25, 30, ____, 40, 45, ____, 55, 60, ____, 70, 75

60, ____, 50, 45, ____, 35, ____, 25, 20, 15, ____, 5

____, 20, ____, 40, 50, 60, ____, 80, ____

10 flowers

Pick the number that tells **about** how many flowers.

Circle the number.

5 40 90

5 40 90

CHAPTER 4 POSTTEST

NAME ____________________

Mid-Test Chapters 1–4

Count how many. Write the number.

____

____

____

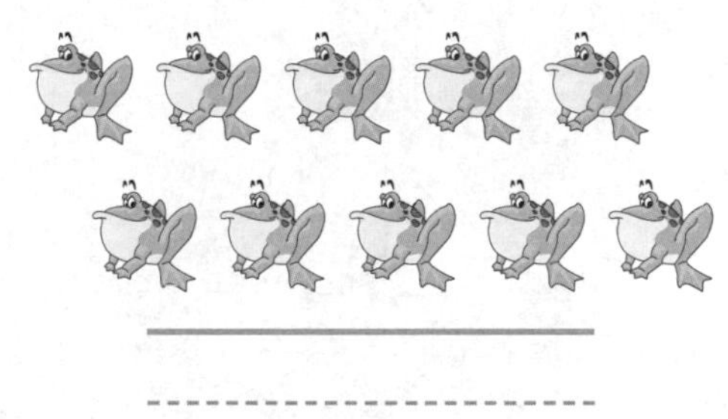

____

Complete.

____ tens ____ ones = ______

____ tens ____ ones = ______

____ tens ____ ones = ______

____ tens ____ ones = ______

CHAPTERS 1–4 MID-TEST

NAME ____________________

Mid-Test Chapters 1–4

◯ the fourth [hippo] from the left. ☐ the eighth  from the right.

◯ the third [bird] from the top.

◯ the second [crow] from the bottom.

Count forward or backward. Write the missing numbers.

96, 95, ____, 93, ____, 91, 90, ____, 88, 87, ____, 85

4, 6, 8, ____, ____, 14, 16, 18, ____, ____, 24, 26

58, ____, 54, 52, ____, 48, 46, ____, ____, 40, 38, 36

____, 75, 70, ____, 60, 55, 50, ____, 40, 35, ____, 25

10, ____, ____, 40, 50, ____, 70, ____, 90

NAME ______________________

Mid-Test Chapters 1–4

Add.

5 + 4	3 + 2	8 + 1	4 + 4	0 + 9	2 + 8
6 + 3	7 + 0	9 + 1	2 + 3	1 + 5	0 + 4
4 + 6	2 + 7	6 + 0	1 + 6	0 + 8	4 + 1
1 + 0	3 + 3	5 + 2	8 + 2	5 + 3	6 + 1
7 + 3	2 + 4	3 + 5	0 + 5	1 + 7	0 + 2
0 + 0	2 + 1	4 + 2	5 + 0	1 + 3	0 + 7
2 + 6	8 + 0	6 + 4	4 + 5	3 + 6	7 + 3

CHAPTERS 1–4 MID-TEST

NAME ______________________________

Mid-Test Chapters 1–4

Subtract.

8 − 6	5 − 4	9 − 1	10 − 7	2 − 0	4 − 2
6 − 3	7 − 6	9 − 5	4 − 4	3 − 1	1 − 0
8 − 2	10 − 8	9 − 9	6 − 5	8 − 4	9 − 3
10 − 4	9 − 6	5 − 2	7 − 4	8 − 8	10 − 3
6 − 1	3 − 3	10 − 2	8 − 0	6 − 4	10 − 1
9 − 7	8 − 5	10 − 10	5 − 3	1 − 1	5 − 0
8 − 3	10 − 0	9 − 2	10 − 6	3 − 2	2 − 2

CHAPTERS 1–4 MID-TEST

NAME ______________________

Mid-Test Chapters 1–4

SHOW YOUR WORK

Solve each problem.

I have .
I find .
How much money do I have? ________¢

There are 6 .
2 more  come.
What is the sum of 6 plus 2? ________

Jerome has 3 .
Carla has 3 .
How many in all? ________

Paula buys  for 2¢.
She buys 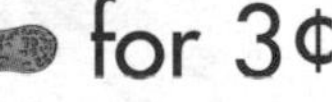 for 3¢.
How much money did she spend? ________¢.

Andy buys  for 7¢.
He buys  for 3¢.
How much money did he spend? ________¢

There is 1 giraffe.
4 more come.
What is 1 + 4? ________.

CHAPTERS 1–4 MID-TEST

Mid-Test Chapters 1–4

SHOW YOUR WORK

Brooke has .
She buys for 1¢.
How much money does she have left? ________¢

____

Drew wants 9 .
He has 4 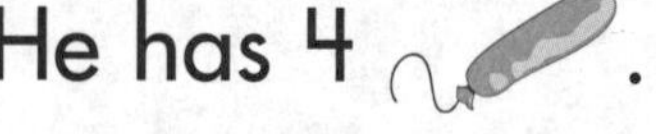.
How many more  does he want? ________

Mike has .
Eva has 8 .
How much more money does Mike have? ________¢

____

Toshi has 4 .
She buys  for 3¢.
How much money does she have left? ________¢

NAME ______________________

Check What You Know

Addition and Subtraction Facts through 18

Add.

5	9	8	6	4	7
+6	+9	+7	+8	+9	+5
8	8	7	8	6	7
+9	+8	+9	+5	+6	+4
9	7	7	9	9	7
+6	+6	+7	+8	+7	+8

Subtract.

15	13	17	16	12	11
− 7	− 9	− 8	− 7	− 6	− 4
14	13	18	15	16	14
− 7	− 6	− 9	− 6	− 8	− 8
12	14	17	16	15	11
− 9	− 6	− 9	− 9	− 8	− 5

NAME ____________________

Check What You Know

SHOW YOUR WORK

Addition and Subtraction Facts through 18

Solve each problem.

There are 8  in a jar.
There are 9  on the table.
How many  in all? ________

There are 12 .
5  swim away.
How many are left? ________

There are 16 on the shelf.
9  roll off.
How many are still on the shelf? ________

There are 6 .
There are 8 .
How many shoes in all? ________

I have 15 .
8  are dirty.
How many  are clean? ________

NAME ____________________

Lesson 5.1 Adding to 11

Add.

$$\begin{array}{r} 7 \\ +4 \\ \hline \end{array}$$

$$\begin{array}{r} 8 \\ +3 \\ \hline \end{array}$$

$$\begin{array}{r} 6 \\ +5 \\ \hline \end{array}$$

$$\begin{array}{r} 9 \\ +2 \\ \hline \end{array}$$

$$\begin{array}{r} 4 \\ +7 \\ \hline \end{array}$$

$$\begin{array}{r} 3 \\ +8 \\ \hline \end{array}$$

$$\begin{array}{r} 5 \\ +6 \\ \hline \end{array}$$

$$\begin{array}{r} 2 \\ +9 \\ \hline \end{array}$$

$$\begin{array}{r} 5 \\ +6 \\ \hline \end{array} \quad \begin{array}{r} 9 \\ +2 \\ \hline \end{array} \quad \begin{array}{r} 4 \\ +7 \\ \hline \end{array} \quad \begin{array}{r} 2 \\ +9 \\ \hline \end{array} \quad \begin{array}{r} 7 \\ +4 \\ \hline \end{array} \quad \begin{array}{r} 8 \\ +3 \\ \hline \end{array}$$

NAME ______________________________

Lesson 5.2 Subtracting from 11

Subtract.

11
− 8
3

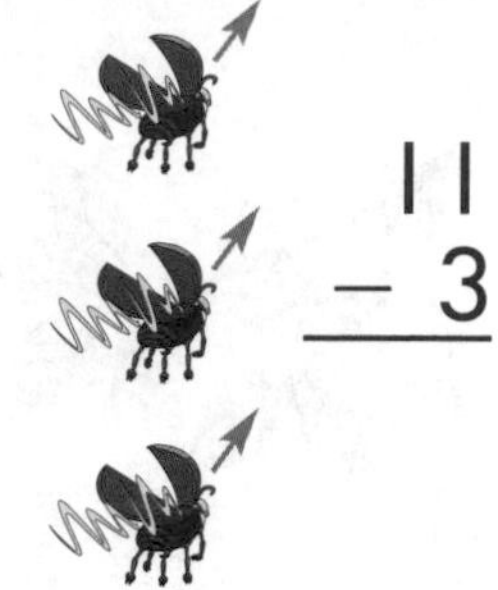

11
− 3

11
− 5

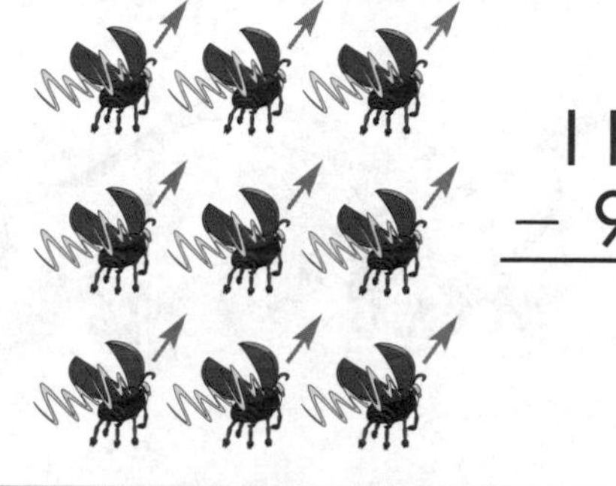

11
− 9

11
− 4

11
− 7

11
− 2

11
− 6

11	11	11	11	11	11
− 3	− 6	− 9	− 8	− 4	− 0

NAME ____________________

Lesson 5.3 Adding to 12

Add.

$\begin{array}{r} 9 \\ +3 \\ \hline 12 \end{array}$

$\begin{array}{r} 3 \\ +9 \\ \hline \end{array}$

$\begin{array}{r} 4 \\ +8 \\ \hline \end{array}$

$\begin{array}{r} 5 \\ +7 \\ \hline \end{array}$

$\begin{array}{r} 7 \\ +5 \\ \hline \end{array}$

$\begin{array}{r} 6 \\ +6 \\ \hline \end{array}$

$\begin{array}{r} 4 \\ +8 \\ \hline \end{array}$ $\quad$ $\begin{array}{r} 8 \\ +4 \\ \hline \end{array}$ $\quad$ $\begin{array}{r} 9 \\ +3 \\ \hline \end{array}$ $\quad$ $\begin{array}{r} 6 \\ +6 \\ \hline \end{array}$ $\quad$ $\begin{array}{r} 3 \\ +9 \\ \hline \end{array}$ $\quad$ $\begin{array}{r} 7 \\ +5 \\ \hline \end{array}$

$5 + 7 =$ ________ $\quad$ $8 + 4 =$ ________ $\quad$ $6 + 6 =$ ________

$9 + 3 =$ ________ $\quad$ $7 + 5 =$ ________ $\quad$ $3 + 9 =$ ________

NAME ____________________

Lesson 5.4 Subtracting from 12

Subtract.

$$\begin{array}{r} 12 \\ -\ 7 \\ \hline 5 \end{array}$$

$$\begin{array}{r} 12 \\ -\ 5 \\ \hline \end{array}$$

$$\begin{array}{r} 12 \\ -\ 6 \\ \hline \end{array}$$

$$\begin{array}{r} 12 \\ -\ 9 \\ \hline \end{array}$$

$$\begin{array}{r} 12 \\ -\ 8 \\ \hline \end{array}$$

$$\begin{array}{r} 12 \\ -\ 3 \\ \hline \end{array}$$

$$\begin{array}{r} 12 \\ -\ 4 \\ \hline \end{array} \quad \begin{array}{r} 12 \\ -\ 3 \\ \hline \end{array} \quad \begin{array}{r} 12 \\ -\ 8 \\ \hline \end{array} \quad \begin{array}{r} 12 \\ -\ 7 \\ \hline \end{array} \quad \begin{array}{r} 12 \\ -\ 6 \\ \hline \end{array} \quad \begin{array}{r} 12 \\ -\ 5 \\ \hline \end{array}$$

$12 - 9 =$ ______ $12 - 8 =$ ______ $12 - 6 =$ ______

$12 - 7 =$ ______ $12 - 3 =$ ______ $12 - 4 =$ ______

Lesson 5.5 Adding to 13

Add.

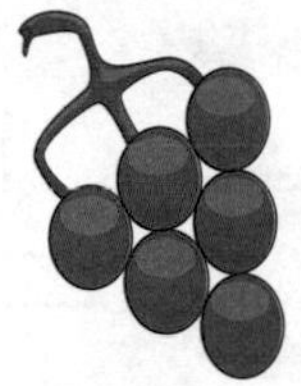
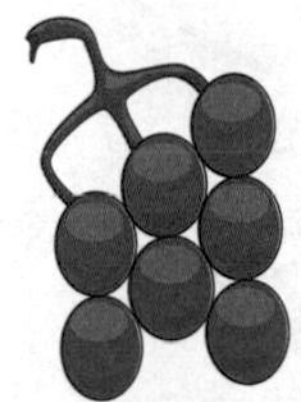

$$\begin{array}{r} 6 \\ +7 \\ \hline 13 \end{array}$$

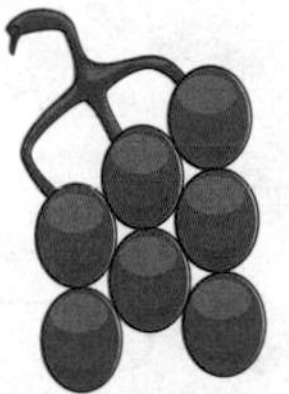
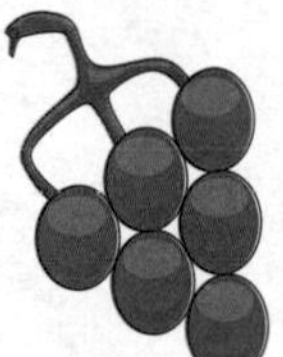

$$\begin{array}{r} 7 \\ +6 \\ \hline \end{array}$$

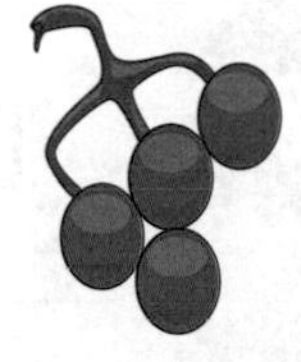
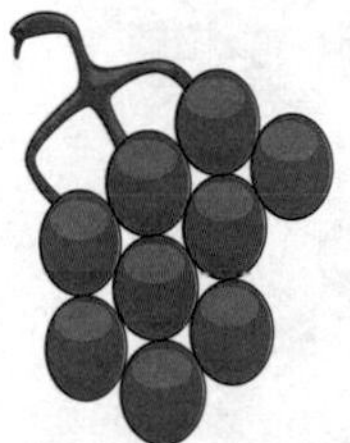

$$\begin{array}{r} 4 \\ +9 \\ \hline \end{array}$$

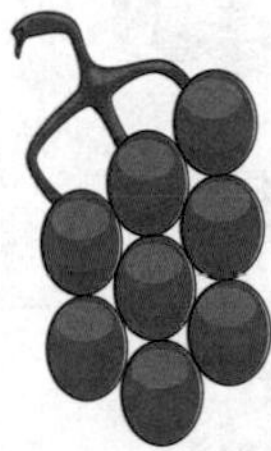
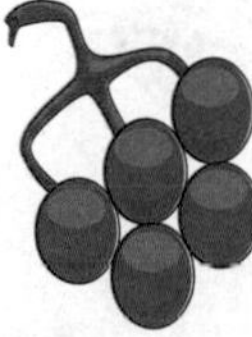

$$\begin{array}{r} 8 \\ +5 \\ \hline \end{array}$$

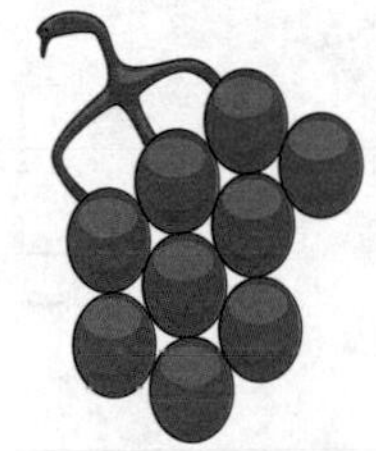
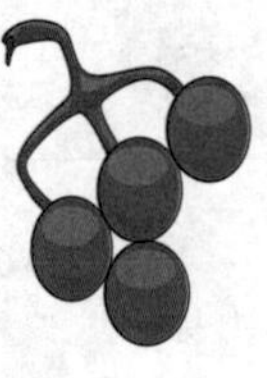

$$\begin{array}{r} 9 \\ +4 \\ \hline \end{array}$$

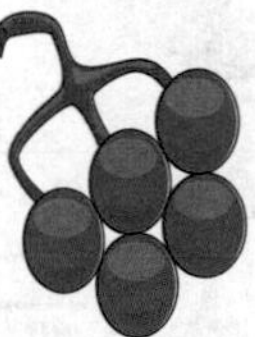
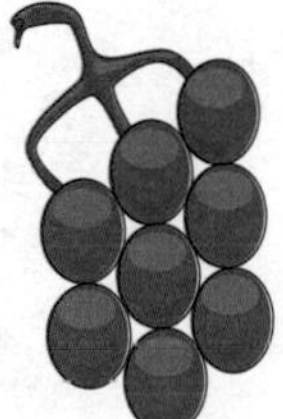

$$\begin{array}{r} 5 \\ +8 \\ \hline \end{array}$$

$$\begin{array}{r} 7 \\ +6 \\ \hline \end{array} \quad \begin{array}{r} 5 \\ +8 \\ \hline \end{array} \quad \begin{array}{r} 9 \\ +4 \\ \hline \end{array} \quad \begin{array}{r} 6 \\ +7 \\ \hline \end{array} \quad \begin{array}{r} 4 \\ +9 \\ \hline \end{array} \quad \begin{array}{r} 8 \\ +5 \\ \hline \end{array}$$

$5 + 8 =$ ________ $4 + 9 =$ ________ $7 + 6 =$ ________

$9 + 4 =$ ________ $8 + 5 =$ ________ $6 + 7 =$ ________

Lesson 5.6 Subtracting from 13

Subtract.

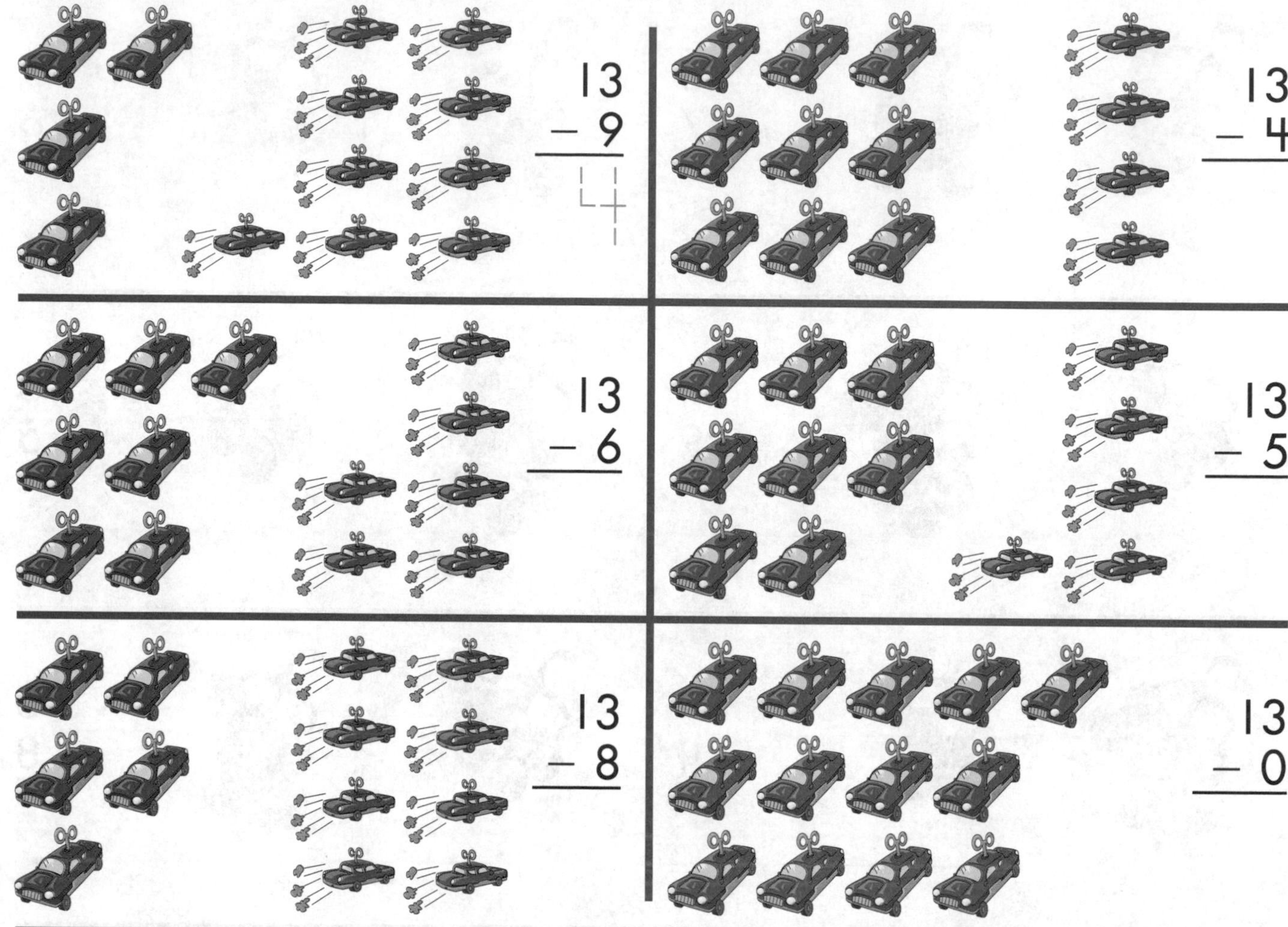

$$\begin{array}{r} 13 \\ -\ 9 \\ \hline 4 \end{array} \qquad \begin{array}{r} 13 \\ -\ 4 \\ \hline \end{array}$$

$$\begin{array}{r} 13 \\ -\ 6 \\ \hline \end{array} \qquad \begin{array}{r} 13 \\ -\ 5 \\ \hline \end{array}$$

$$\begin{array}{r} 13 \\ -\ 8 \\ \hline \end{array} \qquad \begin{array}{r} 13 \\ -\ 0 \\ \hline \end{array}$$

$$\begin{array}{r} 13 \\ -\ 9 \\ \hline \end{array} \quad \begin{array}{r} 13 \\ -\ 8 \\ \hline \end{array} \quad \begin{array}{r} 13 \\ -\ 5 \\ \hline \end{array} \quad \begin{array}{r} 13 \\ -\ 7 \\ \hline \end{array} \quad \begin{array}{r} 13 \\ -\ 0 \\ \hline \end{array} \quad \begin{array}{r} 13 \\ -\ 6 \\ \hline \end{array}$$

$13 - 7 =$ ______ $13 - 8 =$ ______ $13 - 4 =$ ______

$13 - 5 =$ ______ $13 - 9 =$ ______ $13 - 6 =$ ______

Lesson 5.7 Adding to 14

Add.

$$\begin{array}{r} 5 \\ +9 \\ \hline 14 \end{array}$$

$$\begin{array}{r} 9 \\ +5 \\ \hline \end{array}$$

$$\begin{array}{r} 14 \\ +0 \\ \hline \end{array}$$

$$\begin{array}{r} 6 \\ +8 \\ \hline \end{array}$$

$$\begin{array}{r} 7 \\ +7 \\ \hline \end{array}$$

$$\begin{array}{r} 8 \\ +6 \\ \hline \end{array}$$

$$\begin{array}{r} 9 \\ +5 \\ \hline \end{array} \quad \begin{array}{r} 7 \\ +7 \\ \hline \end{array} \quad \begin{array}{r} 5 \\ +9 \\ \hline \end{array} \quad \begin{array}{r} 6 \\ +8 \\ \hline \end{array} \quad \begin{array}{r} 0 \\ +14 \\ \hline \end{array} \quad \begin{array}{r} 8 \\ +6 \\ \hline \end{array}$$

$5 + 8 =$ ________ $7 + 7 =$ ________ $6 + 8 =$ ________

NAME ____________________

Lesson 5.8 Subtracting from 14

Subtract.

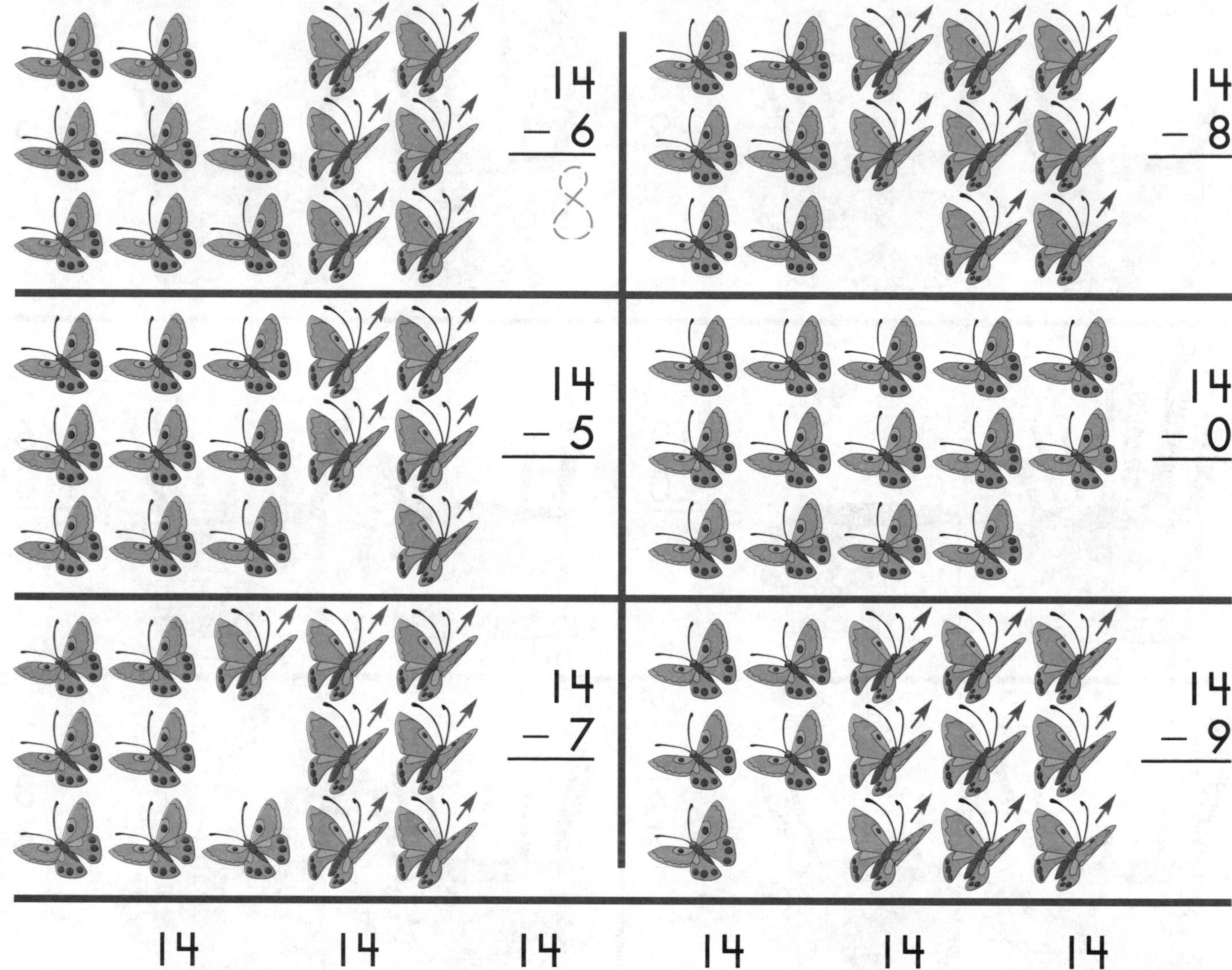

14	14	14	14	14	14
− 0	− 7	− 8	− 9	− 6	− 5

14 − 7 = ______ 14 − 9 = ______ 14 − 6 = ______

14 − 8 = ______ 14 − 2 = ______ 14 − 3 = ______

NAME ______________________

Lesson 5.9 Addition and Subtraction Practice through 14

Add.

6	7	8	6	3	4
+5	+6	+4	+8	+9	+7

5	9	8	6	3	5
+8	+4	+3	+6	+8	+7

7	9	2	8	7	5
+7	+3	+9	+5	+5	+9

Subtract.

14	12	13	11	12	14
− 9	− 3	− 5	− 6	− 7	− 8
5					

11	12	14	13	11	13
− 2	− 5	− 6	− 9	− 8	− 6

13	14	11	12	11	12
− 4	− 7	− 4	− 8	− 5	− 9

NAME ______________________

Lesson 5.9 Problem Solving

SHOW YOUR WORK

Solve each problem.

There are 12 .
6 pop.
How many are left? ___6___

$$\begin{array}{r} 12 \\ -\ 6 \\ \hline 6 \end{array}$$

There are 5 in a basket.
There are 9  in a bowl.
How many  in all? ________

There are 11 .
7  fly away.
How many  are left? ________

There are 7 on the table.
There are 6 in the box.
How many in all? ________

There are 13 .
8   blow away.
What is 13 minus 8? ________

There are 4 .
8 more   come.
What is 4 plus 8? ________

Lesson 5.10 Addition and Subtraction Facts through 15

Add.

6
+9
15

9
+6
15

7	9	6	5	7	6
+8	+5	+9	+8	+7	+7

9	7	8	7	8	4
+6	+6	+7	+7	+6	+9

Subtract.

15
− 9
6

15
− 6

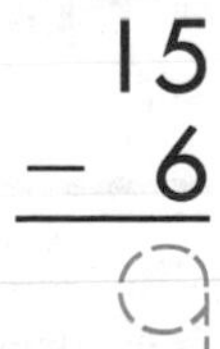

13	15	14	13	14	15
− 7	− 8	− 5	− 8	− 6	− 9

15	13	15	13	14	14
− 7	− 4	− 6	− 9	− 7	− 8

NAME ______________________

Lesson 5.10 Problem Solving

SHOW YOUR WORK

Solve each problem.

There are 15 .

9  drive away.

How many are left? 6

There are 7.

There are 8.

How many leaves in all? ________

There are 9  on the shelf.

There are 6 more  on the floor.

How many  in all? ________

Marcus has 15.

Sue has 7.

How many more  does Marcus have? ________

Len has 15.

He has 6.

How many more  does he have? ________

NAME ______________________

Lesson 5.11 Addition and Subtraction Facts through 16

Add.

$$\begin{array}{r} 7 \\ +9 \\ \hline 16 \end{array}$$

$$\begin{array}{r} 9 \\ +7 \\ \hline 16 \end{array}$$

$\begin{array}{r} 7 \\ +7 \\ \hline \end{array}$ $\begin{array}{r} 8 \\ +8 \\ \hline \end{array}$ $\begin{array}{r} 7 \\ +8 \\ \hline \end{array}$ $\begin{array}{r} 9 \\ +7 \\ \hline \end{array}$ $\begin{array}{r} 5 \\ +9 \\ \hline \end{array}$ $\begin{array}{r} 9 \\ +6 \\ \hline \end{array}$

$\begin{array}{r} 6 \\ +9 \\ \hline \end{array}$ $\begin{array}{r} 6 \\ +8 \\ \hline \end{array}$ $\begin{array}{r} 7 \\ +9 \\ \hline \end{array}$ $\begin{array}{r} 9 \\ +5 \\ \hline \end{array}$ $\begin{array}{r} 8 \\ +6 \\ \hline \end{array}$ $\begin{array}{r} 8 \\ +7 \\ \hline \end{array}$

Subtract.

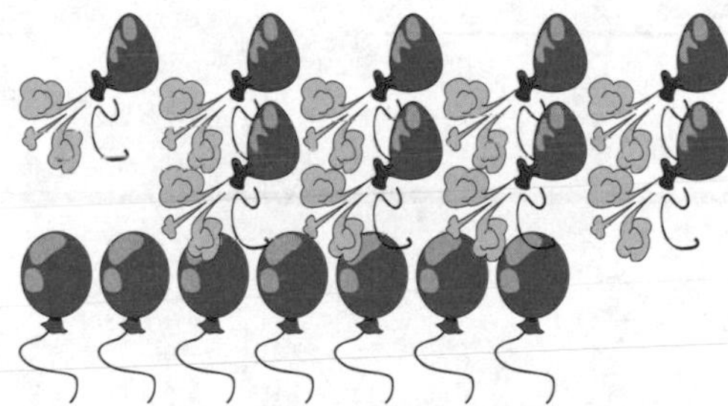

$$\begin{array}{r} 16 \\ -\ 9 \\ \hline 7 \end{array}$$

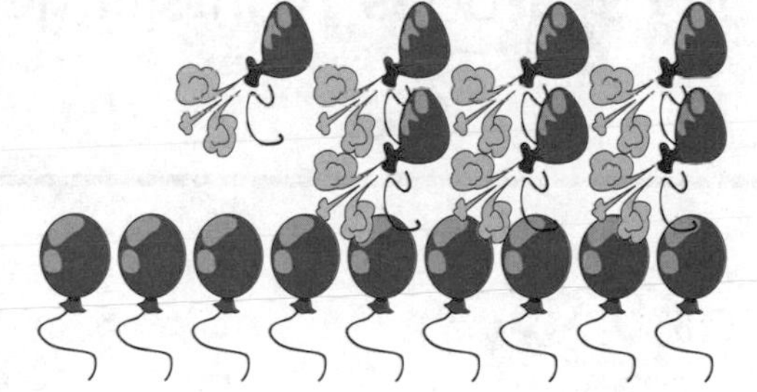

$$\begin{array}{r} 16 \\ -\ 7 \\ \hline 9 \end{array}$$

$\begin{array}{r} 15 \\ -\ 7 \\ \hline \end{array}$ $\begin{array}{r} 16 \\ -\ 8 \\ \hline \end{array}$ $\begin{array}{r} 14 \\ -\ 9 \\ \hline \end{array}$ $\begin{array}{r} 15 \\ -\ 9 \\ \hline \end{array}$ $\begin{array}{r} 14 \\ -\ 7 \\ \hline \end{array}$ $\begin{array}{r} 16 \\ -\ 7 \\ \hline \end{array}$

$\begin{array}{r} 15 \\ -\ 6 \\ \hline \end{array}$ $\begin{array}{r} 14 \\ -\ 8 \\ \hline \end{array}$ $\begin{array}{r} 16 \\ -\ 9 \\ \hline \end{array}$ $\begin{array}{r} 14 \\ -\ 5 \\ \hline \end{array}$ $\begin{array}{r} 15 \\ -\ 8 \\ \hline \end{array}$ $\begin{array}{r} 14 \\ -\ 6 \\ \hline \end{array}$

NAME ______________________

Lesson 5.11 Problem Solving

SHOW YOUR WORK

Solve each problem.

There are 9 .
There are 7 .
How many in all? 16

$$\begin{array}{r} 9 \\ +\ 7 \\ \hline 16 \end{array}$$

There are 16 .
Ted eats 8 .
How many peanuts are left? ________

Ivan has 16 .
He has read 7 .
How many books does Ivan still need to read? ________

Aisha has 8 .
She has 8 .
How many in all? ________

There are 7 .
9 more  come.
How many  are there? ________

NAME ____________________

Lesson 5.12 Addition and Subtraction Facts through 18

Add.

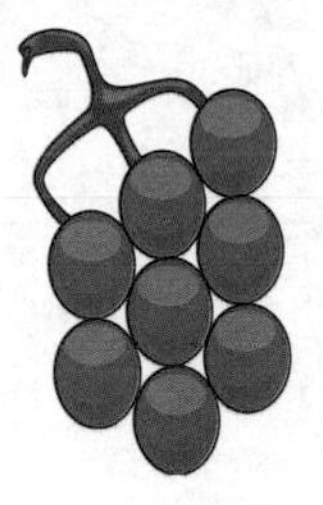 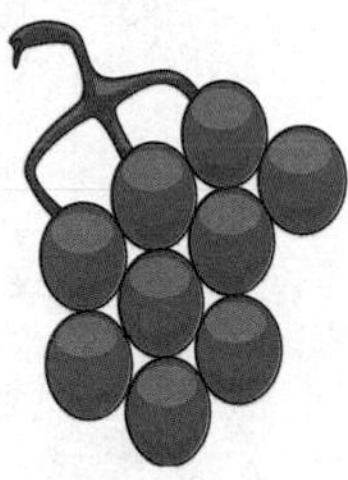

$$\begin{array}{r} 8 \\ +9 \\ \hline 17 \end{array}$$

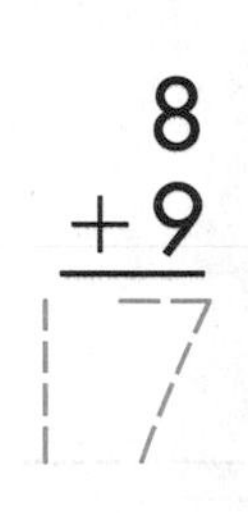 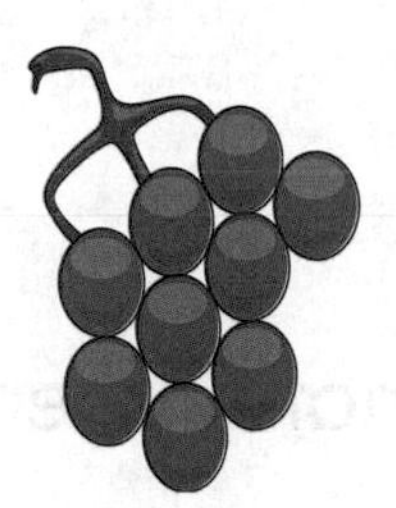 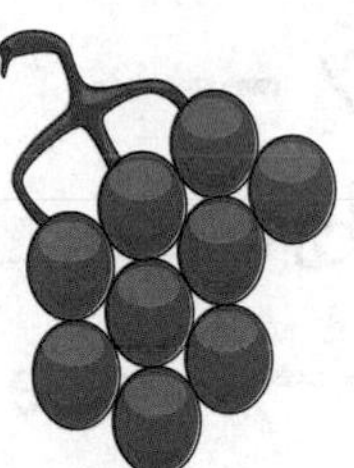

$$\begin{array}{r} 9 \\ +9 \\ \hline 18 \end{array}$$

$$\begin{array}{r} 8 \\ +8 \\ \hline \end{array} \quad \begin{array}{r} 9 \\ +8 \\ \hline \end{array} \quad \begin{array}{r} 5 \\ +9 \\ \hline \end{array} \quad \begin{array}{r} 7 \\ +8 \\ \hline \end{array} \quad \begin{array}{r} 9 \\ +9 \\ \hline \end{array} \quad \begin{array}{r} 8 \\ +6 \\ \hline \end{array}$$

$$\begin{array}{r} 6 \\ +9 \\ \hline \end{array} \quad \begin{array}{r} 7 \\ +7 \\ \hline \end{array} \quad \begin{array}{r} 8 \\ +9 \\ \hline \end{array} \quad \begin{array}{r} 8 \\ +7 \\ \hline \end{array} \quad \begin{array}{r} 9 \\ +7 \\ \hline \end{array} \quad \begin{array}{r} 9 \\ +6 \\ \hline \end{array}$$

Subtract.

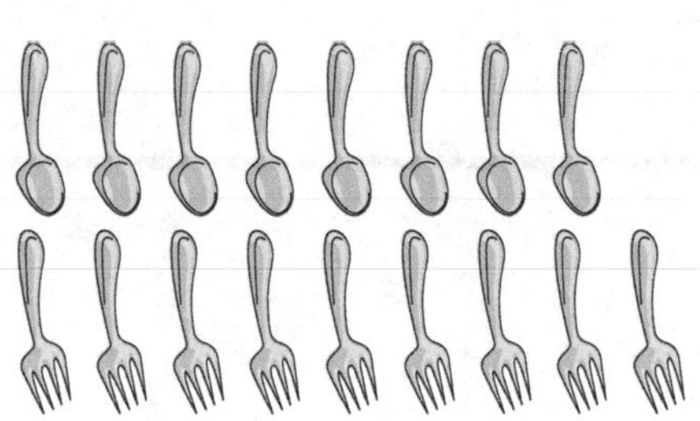

$$\begin{array}{r} 17 \\ -\ 9 \\ \hline 8 \end{array} \quad \begin{array}{r} 17 \\ -\ 8 \\ \hline 9 \end{array}$$

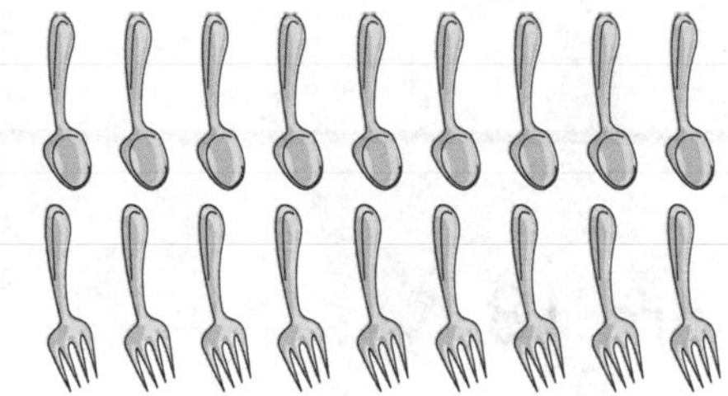

$$\begin{array}{r} 18 \\ -\ 9 \\ \hline 9 \end{array}$$

$$\begin{array}{r} 15 \\ -\ 8 \\ \hline \end{array} \quad \begin{array}{r} 17 \\ -\ 9 \\ \hline \end{array} \quad \begin{array}{r} 14 \\ -\ 7 \\ \hline \end{array} \quad \begin{array}{r} 18 \\ -\ 9 \\ \hline \end{array} \quad \begin{array}{r} 16 \\ -\ 7 \\ \hline \end{array} \quad \begin{array}{r} 15 \\ -\ 6 \\ \hline \end{array}$$

$$\begin{array}{r} 17 \\ -\ 8 \\ \hline \end{array} \quad \begin{array}{r} 14 \\ -\ 6 \\ \hline \end{array} \quad \begin{array}{r} 16 \\ -\ 9 \\ \hline \end{array} \quad \begin{array}{r} 16 \\ -\ 8 \\ \hline \end{array} \quad \begin{array}{r} 15 \\ -\ 7 \\ \hline \end{array} \quad \begin{array}{r} 14 \\ -\ 5 \\ \hline \end{array}$$

NAME ________________

Lesson 5.12 Problem Solving

SHOW YOUR WORK

Solve each problem.

There are 17 pencils.
9 pencils are broken.
How many pencils are not broken? 8

$$\begin{array}{r} 17 \\ -\ 9 \\ \hline 8 \end{array}$$

There are 9 ladybugs.
9 more ladybugs come.
How many ladybugs are there? ________

Luisa caught 8 fish.
She catches 9 more fish.
How many fish did she catch in all? ________

There are 18 rabbits.
9 rabbits run away.
How many rabbits are left? ________

There are 17 shovels.
There are 8 rakes.
How many more shovels are there? ________

Lesson 5.13 Addition and Subtraction Practice through 18

Add.

9	9	6	7	8	7
+8	+7	+9	+8	+5	+7
17					

9	7	8	8	8	9
+9	+9	+7	+9	+6	+4

7	9	9	8	6	6
+6	+5	+6	+8	+8	+7

Subtract.

14	15	16	13	15	17
− 9	− 7	− 8	− 6	− 8	− 9
5					

18	16	14	13	15	17
− 9	− 7	− 8	− 4	− 6	− 8

16	13	14	15	14	13
− 9	− 8	− 7	− 9	− 5	− 7

NAME ______________________

Lesson 5.13 Problem Solving

SHOW YOUR WORK

Solve each problem.

There are 17 crows.
Nine crows fly away.
How many are left? 8

$$\begin{array}{r} 17 \\ -\ 9 \\ \hline 8 \end{array}$$

I have 9 bananas.
I have 6 oranges.
What is the sum? ________

There are 18 juice boxes.
We drink 9 juice boxes.
How many are left? ________

There are 8 cars.
8 more cars drive up.
How many cars are there in all? ________

I want 16 pencils.
I have 7 pencils.
How many more do I need? ________

NAME ______________________________

Check What You Learned

Addition and Subtraction Facts through 18

Add.

8	8	6	7	3	9
+7	+9	+7	+4	+8	+5

9	5	7	6	8	9
+3	+8	+9	+6	+4	+9

7	7	4	2	6	8
+5	+8	+9	+9	+9	+6

Subtract.

14	15	13	12	16	11
− 5	− 7	− 8	− 4	− 9	− 3

17	14	12	13	11	18
− 8	− 7	− 6	− 5	− 7	− 9

13	15	16	17	12	11
− 9	− 8	− 7	− 9	− 8	− 5

Check What You Learned

SHOW YOUR WORK

Addition and Subtraction Facts through 18

CHAPTER 5 POSTTEST

Solve each problem.

There are 14 .
There are 8 .
What is the difference? ________

There are 7 .
There are 6 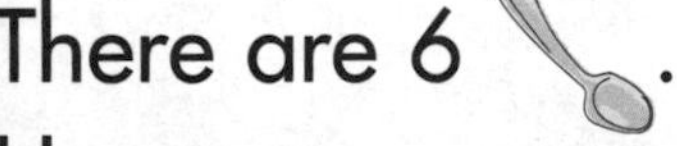.
How many spoons in all? ________

There are 18 .
We eat 9 .
How many are left? ________

There are 6 .
9 more  come.
How many  are there in all? ________

Tanya has 9 .
Curtis has 7 .
How many do they have in all? ________

NAME ______________________

Check What You Know

Measurement

Count and write how much money.

________ ¢

________ ¢

________ ¢

________ ¢

Write the time for each clock.

_____:00

_____ o'clock

_____:30

_____ thirty

_____:30

_____ thirty

Look at the calendar.

April						
Sun.	Mon.	Tues.	Wed.	Thurs.	Fri.	Sat.
	1	2	3	4	5	6
7	8	9	10	11	12	13
14	15	16	17	18	19	20
21	22	23	24	25	26	27
28	29	30				

What day is April 8? ____________

How many Wednesdays are there in April? ____

What day is the first day of April? ____________

What day comes after Friday? ______________

What day is April 25? ________________

NAME ______________________

Check What You Know

Measurement

Use paper clips to measure.

_____ paper clips

_____ paper clips

Circle the heavier object.

Circle the lighter object.

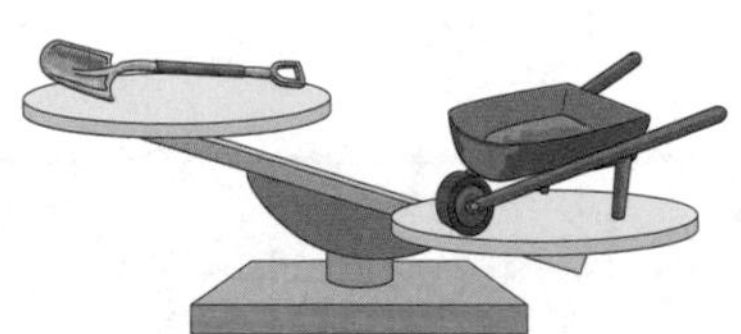

Circle the object that holds more.

Look at the picture graph.

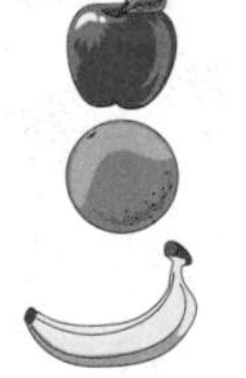

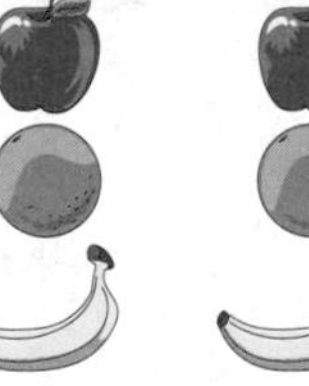
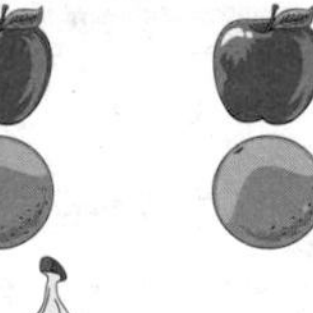

1 2 3 4 5 6 7 8 9 10

Circle your answer.

Which is more?  

Which is fewer?  

NAME ______________________

Lesson 6.1 Money

1 penny	1 nickel	1 dime	1 quarter

1¢	5¢	10¢	25¢

Count and write how much money.

25 ¢

______ ¢

______ ¢

______ ¢

______ ¢

______ ¢

______ ¢

______ ¢

NAME ______________________

Lesson 6.1 Money

1 penny	1 nickel	1 dime	1 quarter

1¢	5¢	10¢	25¢

Count and write how much money.

76 ¢

______ ¢

______ ¢

______ ¢

______ ¢

______ ¢

______ ¢

______ ¢

Lesson 6.2 Telling Time to the Hour

11:00

11 o'clock

Both clocks show the same time.

Write the time for each clock.

4 : 00

4 o'clock

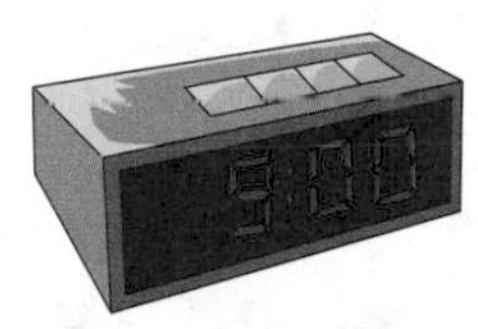

_____ : _____

_____ o'clock

_____ : _____

_____ o'clock

_____ : _____

_____ o'clock

_____ : _____

_____ o'clock

_____ : _____

_____ o'clock

_____ : _____

_____ o'clock

_____ : _____

_____ o'clock

Lesson 6.2 Telling Time to the Hour

What time is it on the first clock?

Write this time on the second clock.

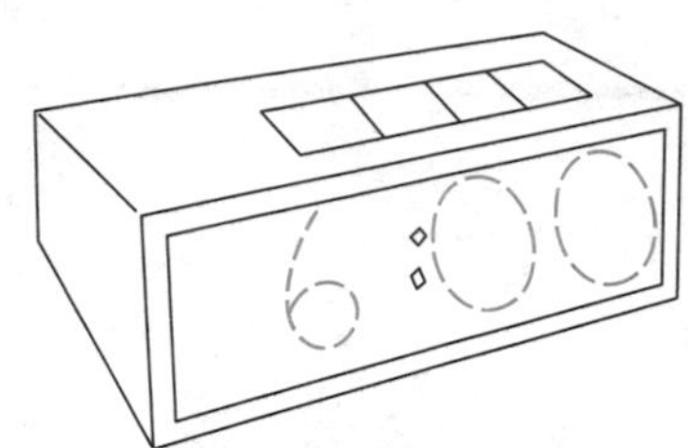

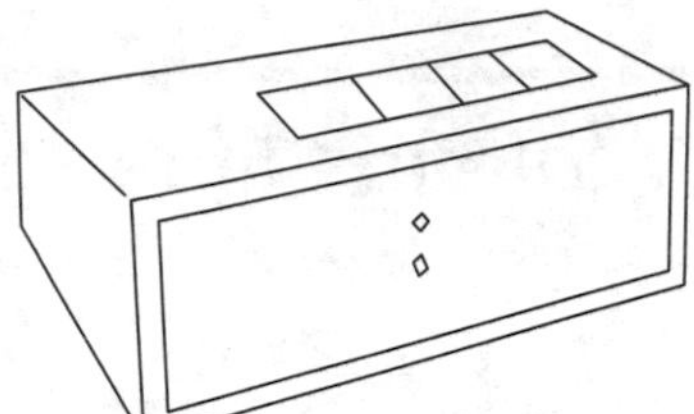

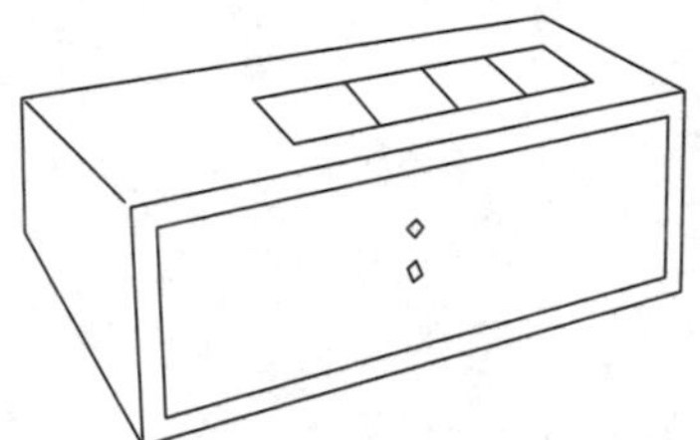

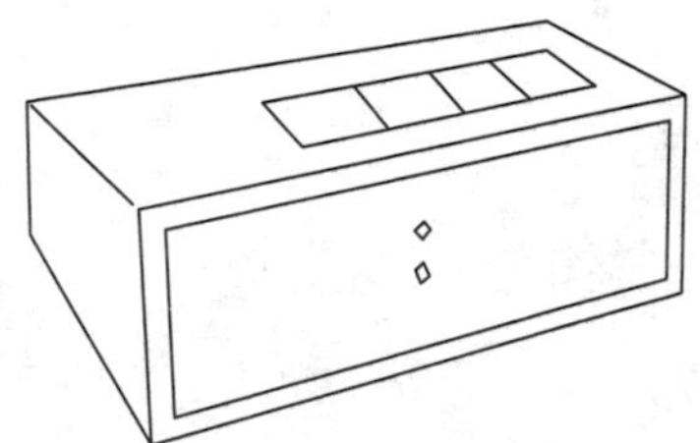

What time is it on the first clock?

Draw the hands to show this time on the second clock.

NAME ______________________

Lesson 6.3 Telling Time to the Half Hour

3:00
3 o'clock

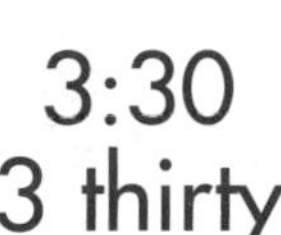

3:30
3 thirty

Write the time for each clock.

1 : 30

1 thirty

_____ : _____

_____ thirty

_____ : _____

_____ thirty

_____ : _____

_____ thirty

_____ : _____

_____ thirty

_____ : _____

_____ thirty

_____ : _____

_____ thirty

_____ : _____

_____ thirty

NAME ____________________

Lesson 6.3 Telling Time to the Half Hour

What time is it on the first clock?

Write this time on the second clock.

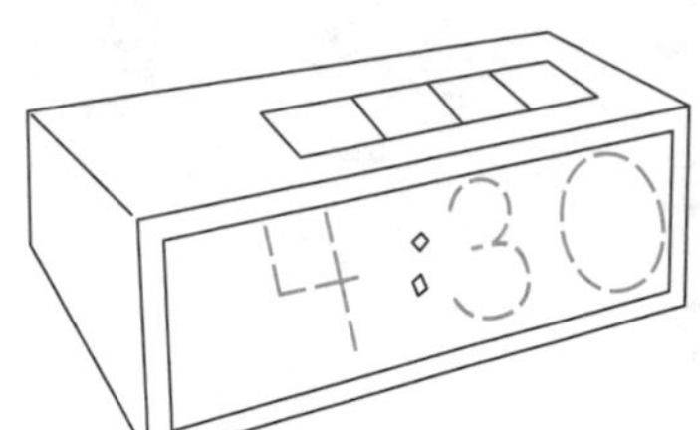

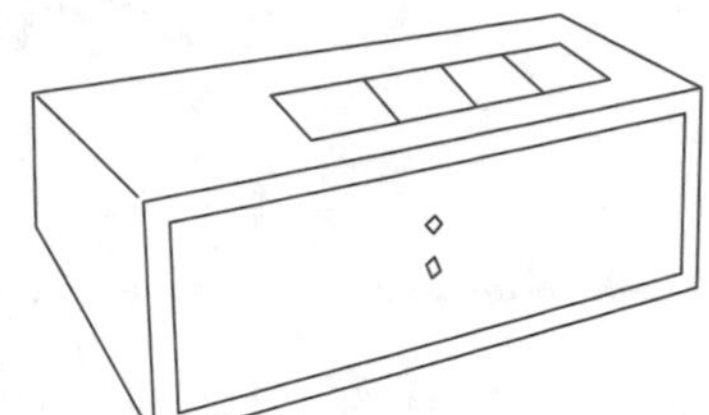

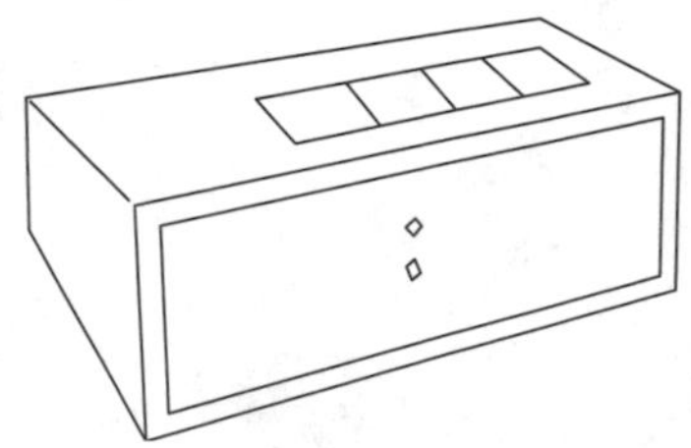

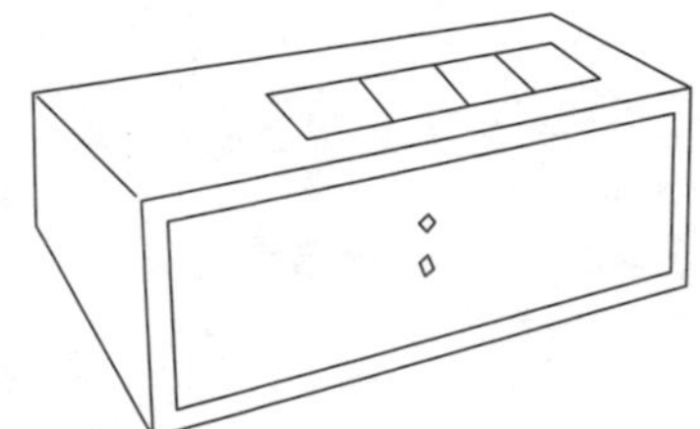

What time is it on the first clock?

Draw the hands to show this time on the second clock.

NAME ______________________________

Lesson 6.4 Reading the Calendar

There are 7 days in a week.
Sunday, Monday, Tuesday, Wednesday, Thursday, Friday, Saturday

June						
Sun.	Mon.	Tues.	Wed.	Thurs.	Fri.	Sat.
		1	2	3	4	5
6	7	8	9	10	11	12
13	14	15	16	17	18	19
20	21	22	23	24	25	26
27	28	29	30			

July						
Sun.	Mon.	Tues.	Wed.	Thurs.	Fri.	Sat.
				1	2	3
4	5	6	7	8	9	10
11	12	13	14	15	16	17
18	19	20	21	22	23	24
25	26	27	28	29	30	31

Look at the calendars. June 1 is on Tuesday. July 1 is on Thursday.

Complete.

What day comes after Tuesday? ______________________________

What day is June 13? ______________________________

July 23 is on ______________________________.

How many Sundays are there in June? ______________________________

What is the last day of June? ______________________________

What day comes between Sunday and Tuesday? ______________________________

What day is July 28? ______________________________

June 26 is on ______________________________.

NAME ______________________

Lesson 6.4 Reading the Calendar

There are 12 months in a year.

Month	January	February	March	April	May	June
Number of Days	31	28	31	30	31	30
Month	July	August	September	October	November	December
Number of Days	31	31	30	31	30	31

Complete.

What is the first month of the year? ______________________

What month comes before June? ______________________

What is the shortest month? ______________________

How many months have 30 days? ______________________

How many months have 31 days? ______________________

What is the last month of the year? ______________________

What month comes after August? ______________________

What month is between March and May? ______________________

NAME ____________________

Lesson 6.5 Measuring Length and Height

Use dimes to measure.

__7__ dimes

Use dimes to measure each object.

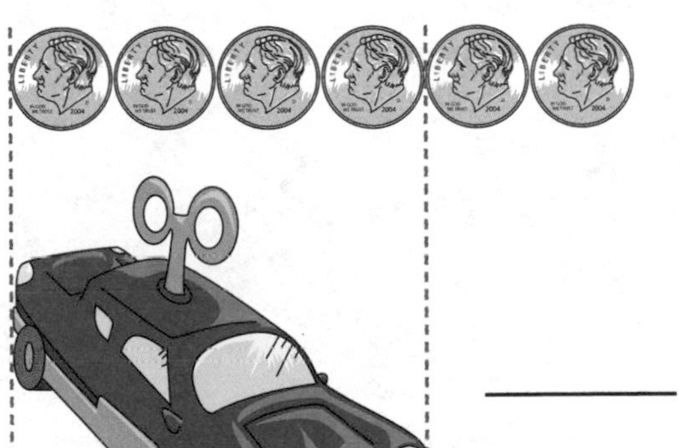

______ dimes

______ dimes

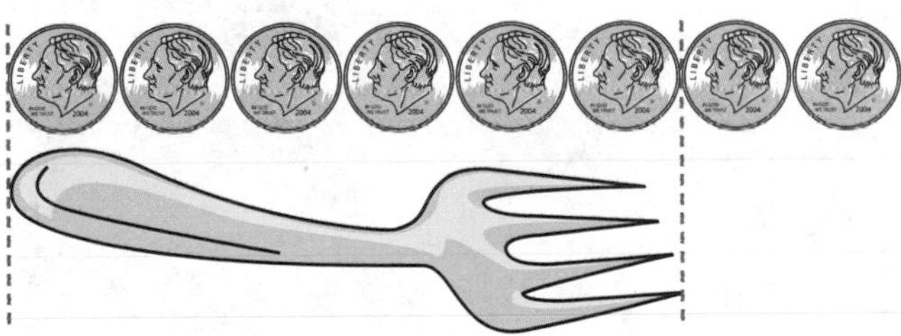

______ dimes

______ dimes

______ dimes

NAME ______________________

Lesson 6.5 Measuring Length and Height

Use paper clips to measure.

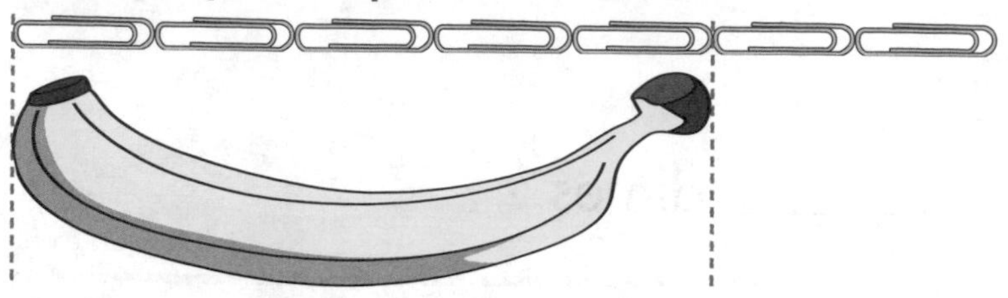

5 paper clips

Use the paper clips to measure each object.

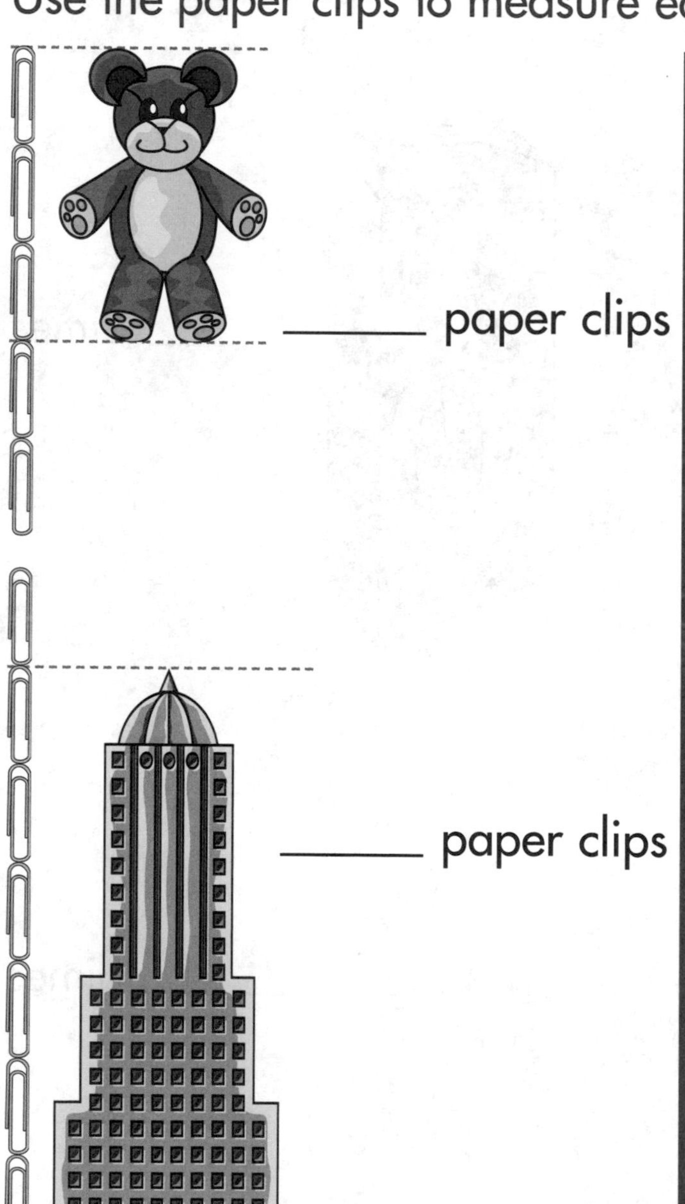

______ paper clips

______ paper clips

______ paper clips

______ paper clips

NAME ______________________________

Lesson 6.6 Measuring Weight

When a balance scale is level, the two sides have the same weight.

How much does each object weigh?

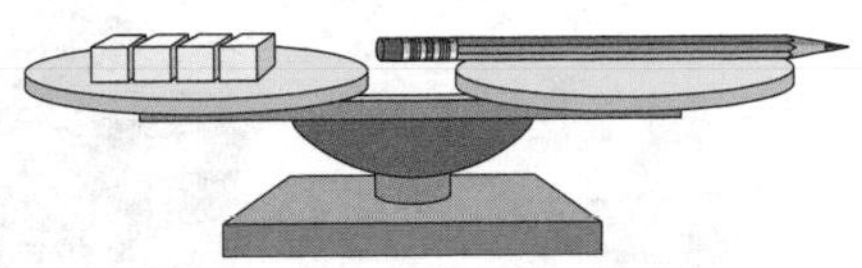

= 4 cubes

= ________ cubes

= ________ cubes

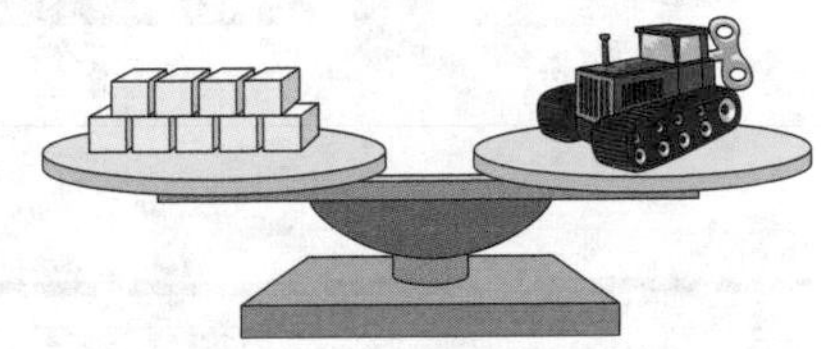

= ________ cubes

Circle the heavier object.

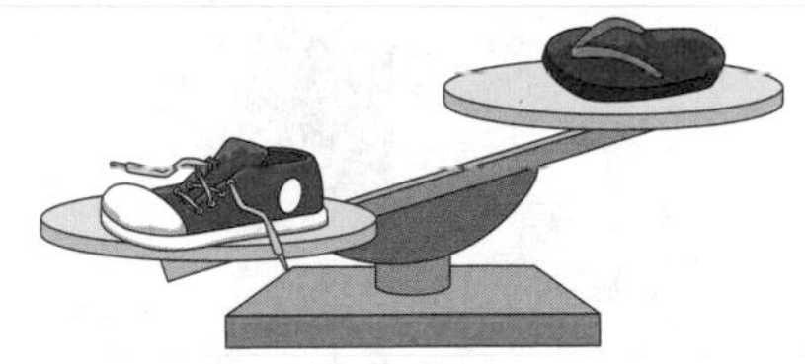

Circle the lighter object.

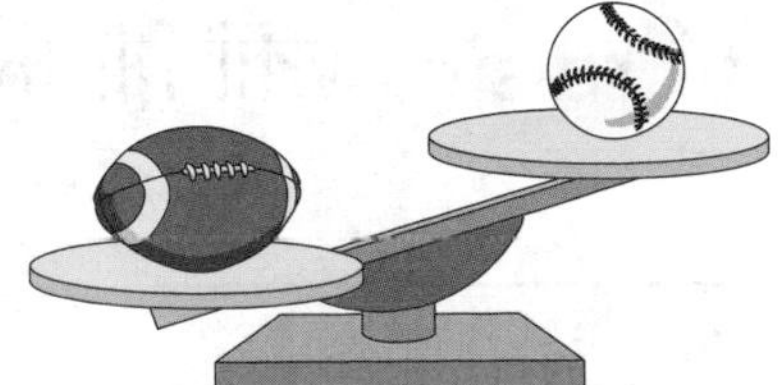

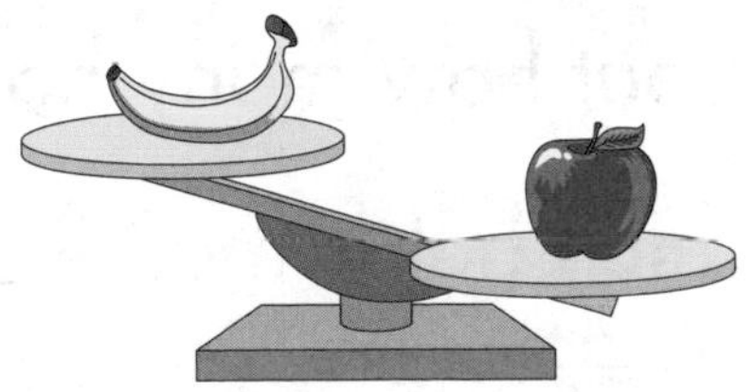

NAME ______________________________

Lesson 6.7 Measuring Volume

Circle the object that holds more.

Circle the object that holds less.

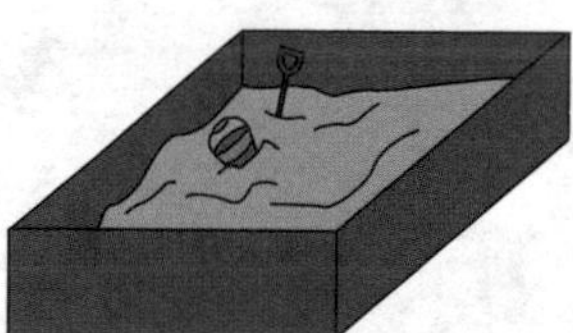

Complete.

About how many boxes of raisins will fill the bowl? __________

About how many boxes of raisins will fill the bag? __________

Which holds more? ____________________

NAME ______________________

Lesson 6.8 More, Less, Fewer

Look at the picture graph.

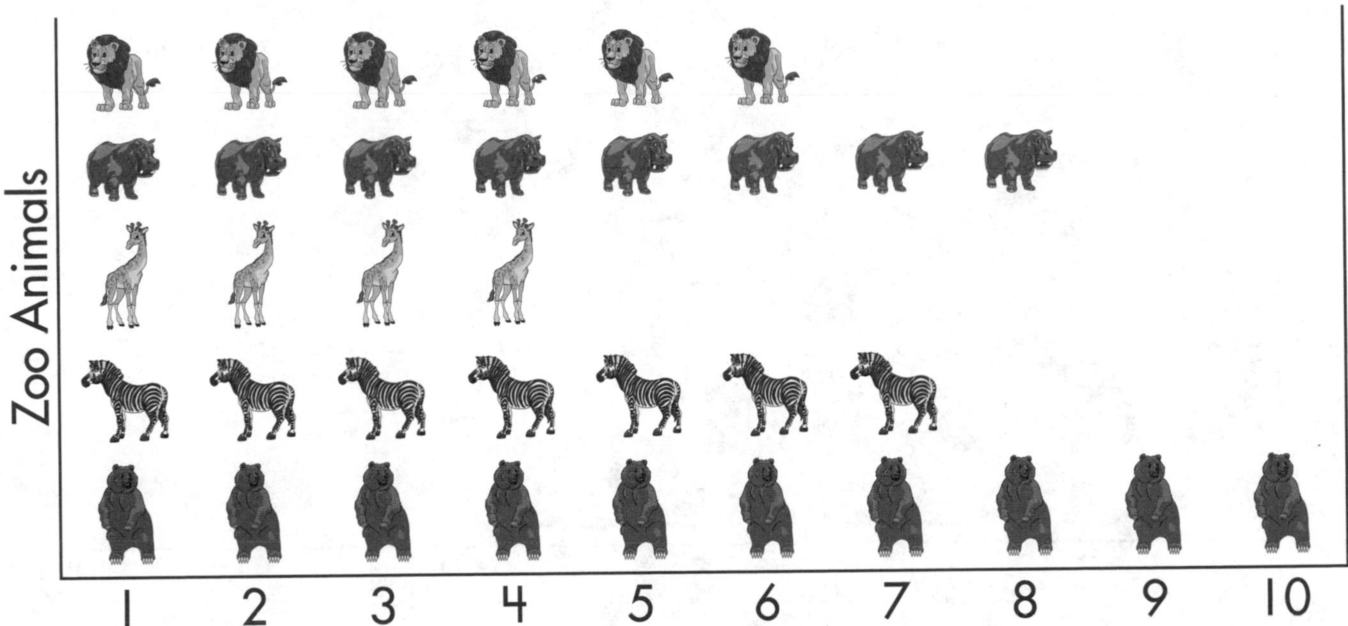

Circle the one that has more.  

Circle the one that has fewer.  

How many  ? ____________

How many  ? ____________

How many  ? ____________

How many  ? ____________

How many  ? ____________

Lesson 6.9 Greater Than, Less Than, and Equal To

Look at the picture graph.

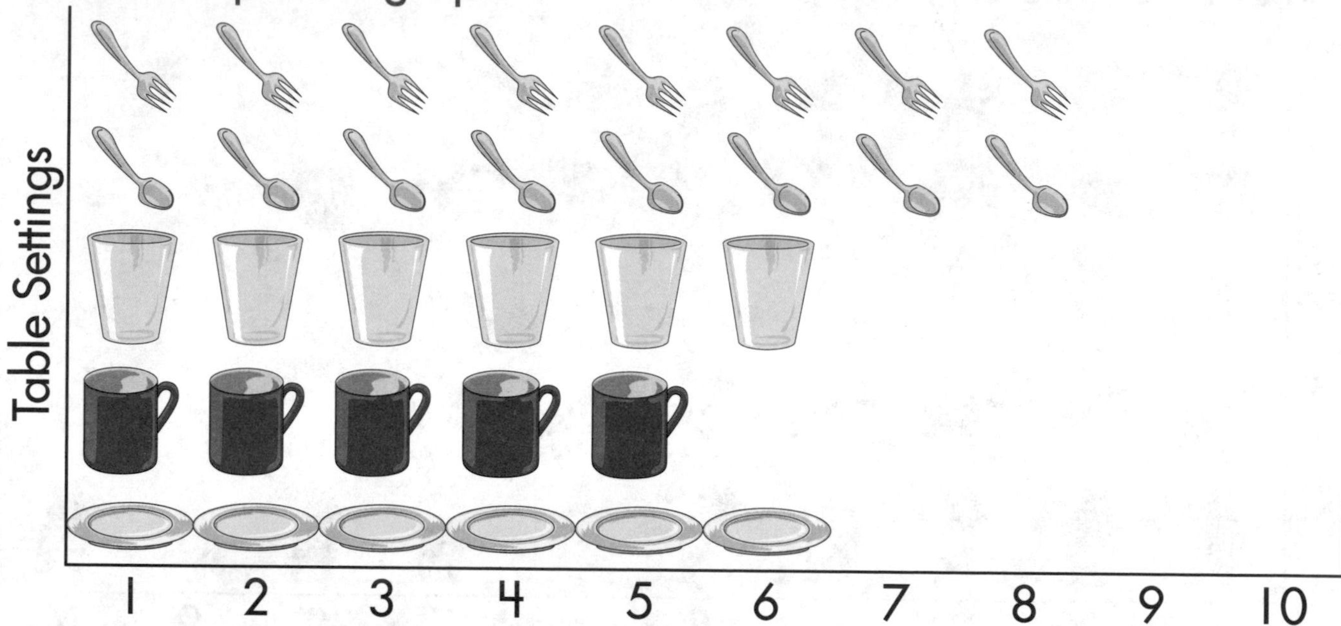

Circle the object that is greater than .

Circle the object that is less than .

Circle the object that is equal to .

Circle the object that is equal to .

Fill in the ________ with *greater than, less than,* or *equal to.*

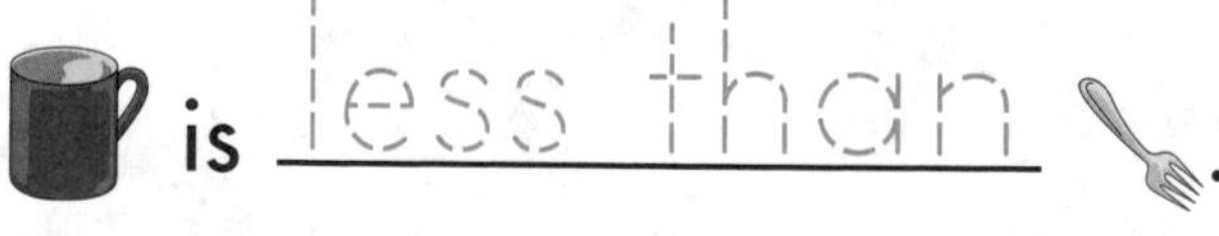

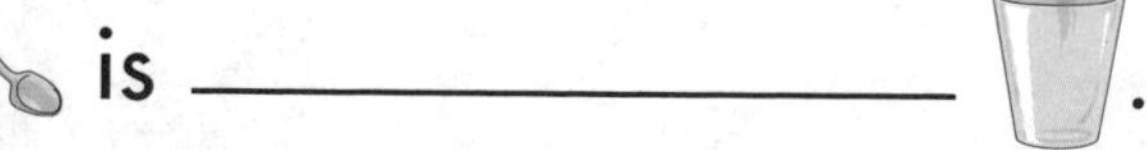

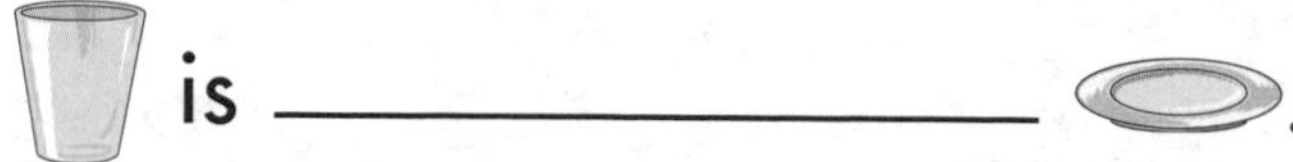

NAME ____________________

Lesson 6.10 Collecting Data

Make a food chart for one day. Show what you ate.

Fruit 

Vegetable 

Meat/Eggs/Fish 

Bread/Cereal 

Other Foods 

Breakfast	
Lunch	
Dinner	
Snacks	

Use your food chart.

How many of each did you eat?

Fruit ________ Bread/Cereal ________

Vegetable ________ Other Foods ________

Meat/Eggs/Fish ________

What food did you eat the most? ________________

At which meal did you eat the most? ________________

What is your favorite food? ________________

NAME ____________________

Lesson 6.10 Collecting Data

Make a pet chart. Ask 20 people if they have a pet.

Use tally marks to show what kind.

Tally Marks
| = 1
|| = 2
||| = 3
|||| = 4
~~||||~~ = 5

				Other	None

Use your pet chart. Write the number.

How many people have  ? ________

How many people have  ? ________

How many people have  ? ________

How many people have  ? ________

How many people do not have a pet? ________

How many people have a pet that is not on the chart? ________

Complete.

Which pet is the favorite? ________________

Which pet is the least favorite? ________________

NAME ____________________

Check What You Learned

Measurement

Count and write how much money.

______ ¢

______ ¢

______ ¢

______ ¢

Write the time for each clock.

____:30

______ thirty

____:30

______ thirty

____:00

______ o'clock

August						
Sun.	Mon.	Tues.	Wed.	Thurs.	Fri.	Sat.
			1	2	3	4
5	6	7	8	9	10	11
12	13	14	15	16	17	18
19	20	21	22	23	24	25
26	27	28	29	30	31	

Look at the calendar.

What day is August 5? ______

What day is August 15? ______

What is the last day of August? ______

What day comes before Monday? ______

How many Tuesdays are there in August? ______

NAME ______________________

Check What You Learned

Measurement

Use paper clips to measure.

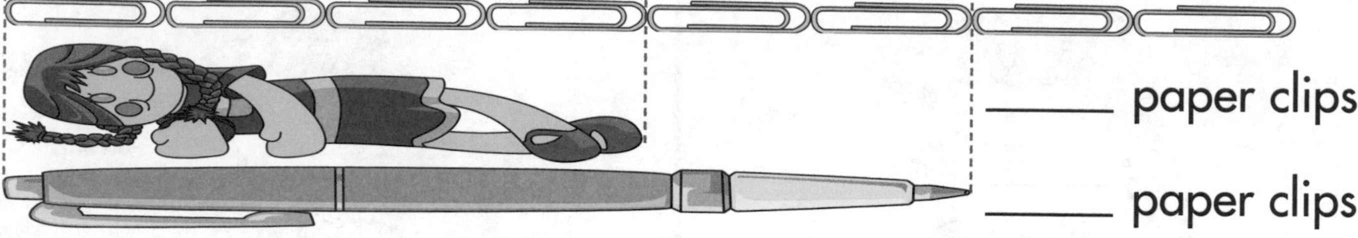

_____ paper clips

_____ paper clips

Circle the lighter object.

Circle the heavier object.

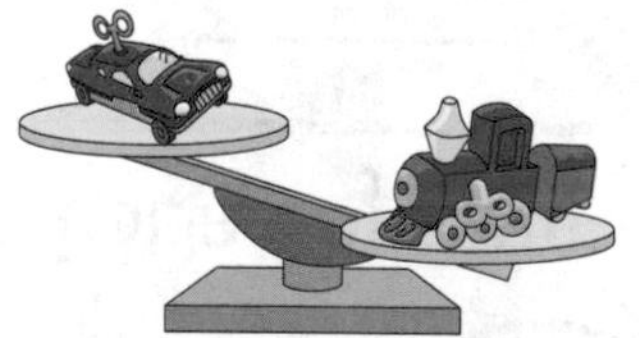

Look at the picture graph.

Fill in the ________ with *greater than, less than,* or *equal to.*

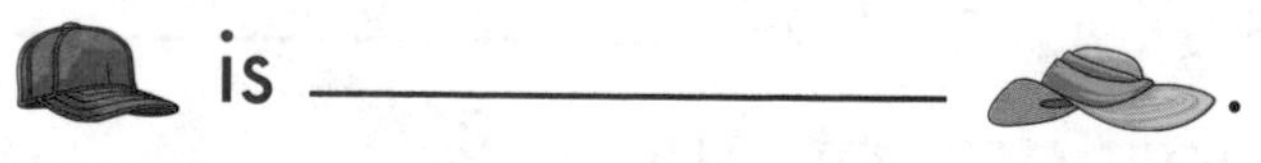

is ______________ .

is ______________ .

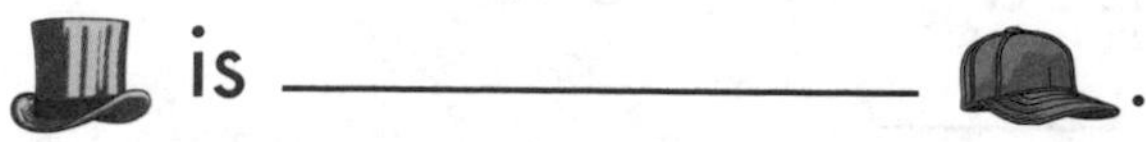

is ______________ .

NAME ____________________

Check What You Know

Geometry

Look at the picture. Circle the object.

What is next to  ?  

What is above  ?  

What is up on the shelf?  

What is below  ?  

What is far from  ?  

What is on the floor?  

What is beside  ? 

NAME ______________________

Check What You Know

Geometry

CHAPTER 7 PRETEST

Write the name of each shape.

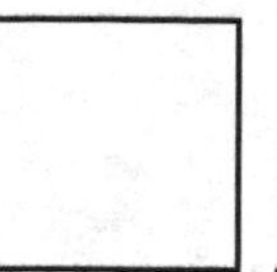

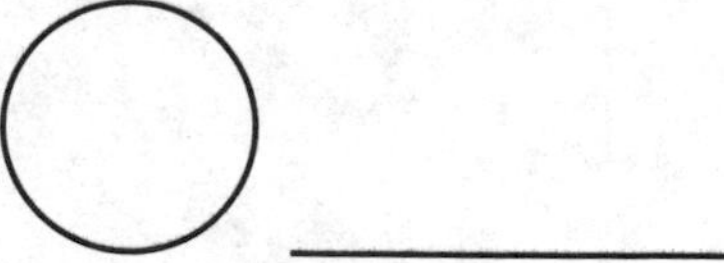

Draw the shape.

Circle
It is a closed curve.

Rectangle
It has 4 sides.

Triangle
It has 3 angles.

Write the name of the shape. Then, draw the shape.

____

____

NAME ______________________

Lesson 7.1 Near and Far; Below and Above

Circle above .

Square below .

Circle above .

Square below .

Circle the animals that are near the house.

Square the animals that are far from the house.

NAME ____________________

Lesson 7.1 Near and Far; Below and Above

Look at the toy shelves.

Write *above* or *below* on the ________.

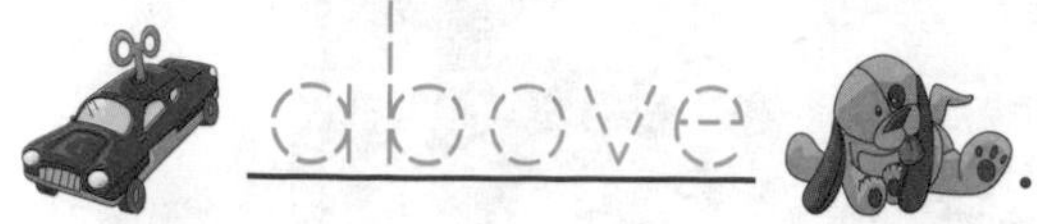

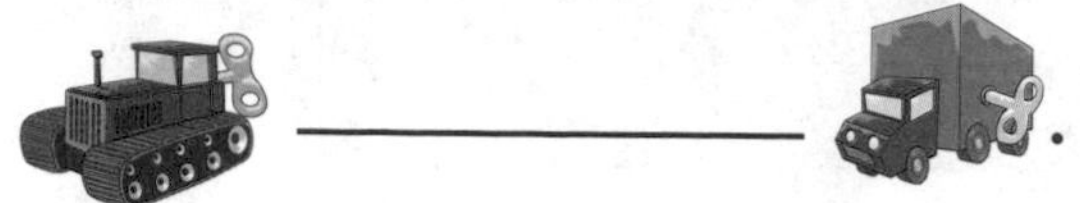

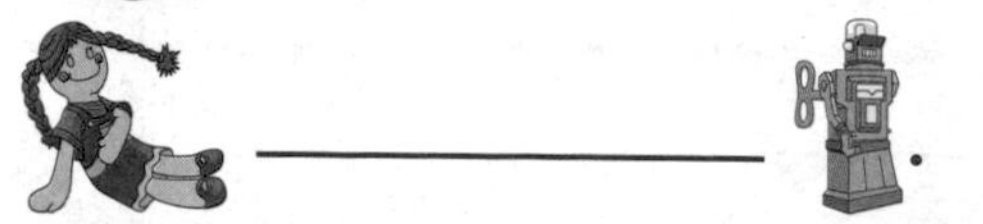

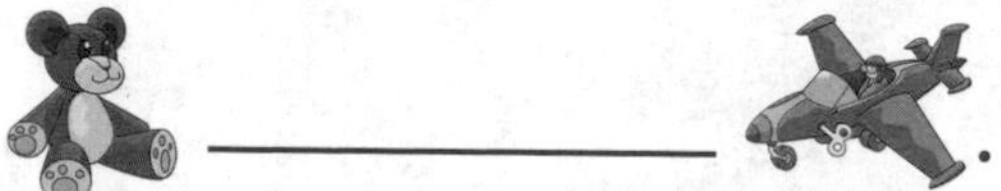

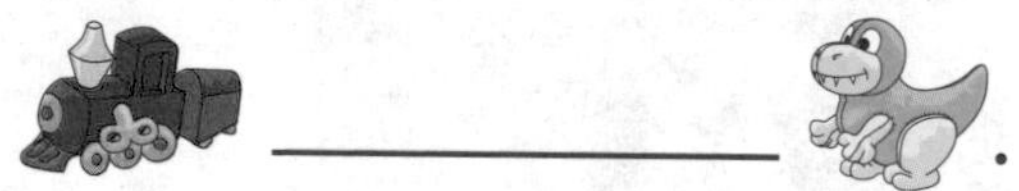

Look at the picture.

Write *near* or *far* on the ________.

near ________.

________.

________.

________.

________.

NAME ____________________

Lesson 7.2 Up and Down; Beside and Next To

 is beside .

 is next to .

These are words that mean the same thing.

 is up in the tree.

 is down on the ground.

Circle the objects up on the table.
Square the objects down on the floor.

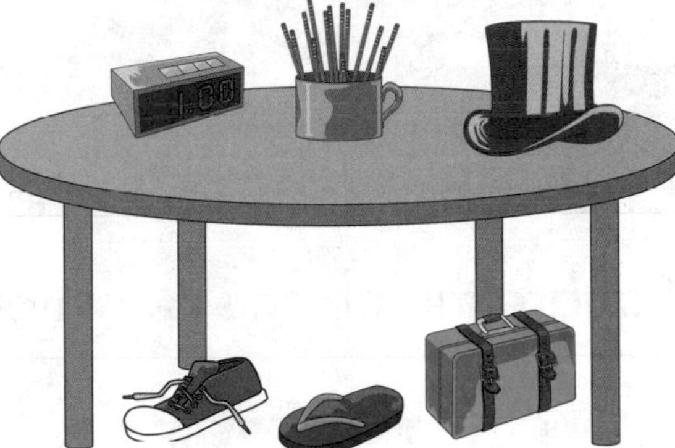

Look at the row of fruit.

     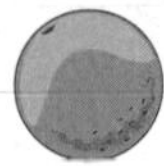   

Circle the  next to .

Circle the  beside .

Circle the  beside .

Circle the  next to .

NAME ____________________

Lesson 7.2 Up and Down; Beside and Next To

Circle the objects up in the air.

Square the objects down on the ground.

Look at the row of animals.

Circle the next to .

Circle the beside .

Circle the beside .

Circle the next to .

NAME ____________________

Lesson 7.3 Identifying Shapes

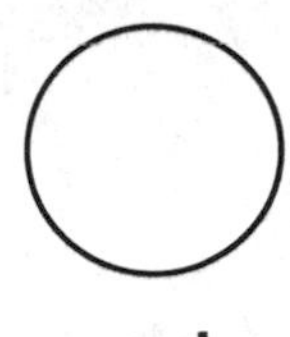
circle

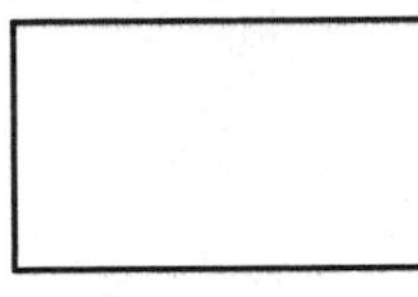
rectangle

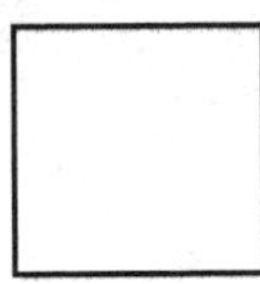
square

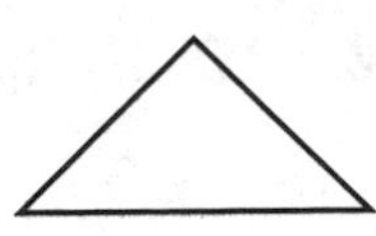
triangle

Write the letter C in all the circles.
Write the letter R in all the rectangles.
Write the letter S in all the squares.
Write the letter T in all the triangles.

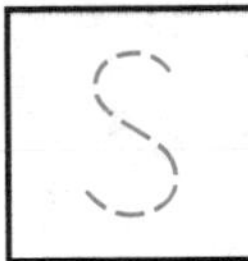

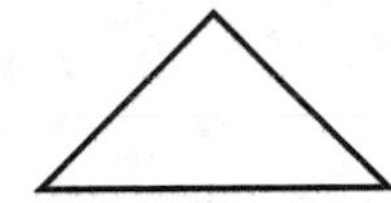

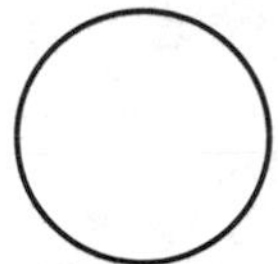

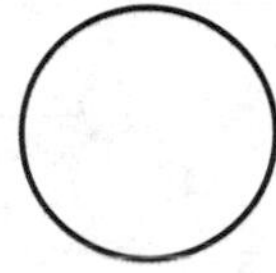
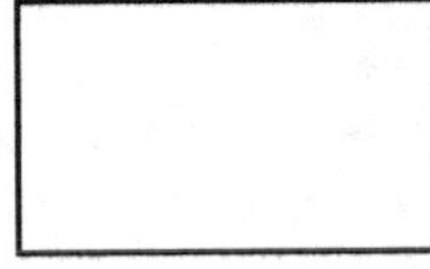
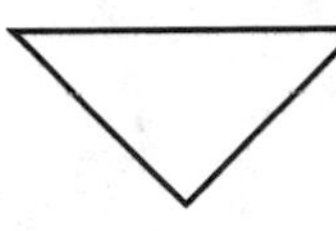

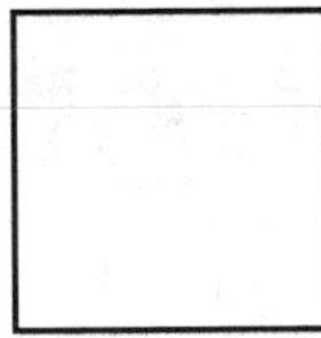
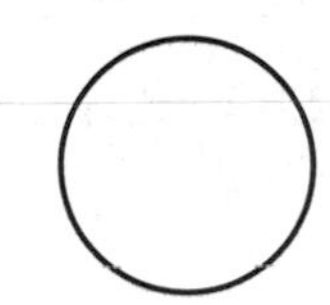

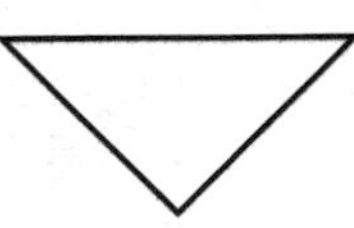

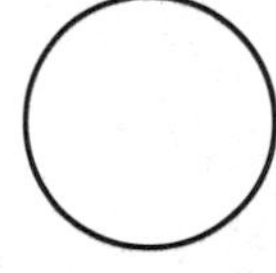

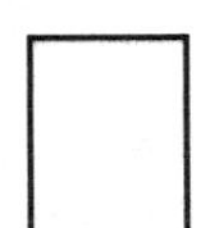

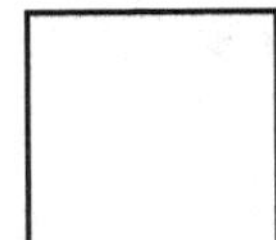

NAME ______________________

Lesson 7.4 Drawing Shapes

Draw the shape.

Rectangle
It has 4 sides.

Circle
It is a closed curve.

Triangle
It has 3 sides.

Square
It has 4 sides.
The sides are the same length.

Triangle
It has 3 angles.

Rectangle
It has 4 sides.

NAME ________________

Lesson 7.5 Finding Shapes

Write the name of each shape. Then, draw the shape.

circle

____

____

____

____

NAME ________________

Lesson 7.5 Finding Shapes

Write the name of each shape. Then, draw the shape.

triangle

____

____

____

____

NAME ____________________

Check What You Learned

Geometry

Look at the picture. Circle the correct object.

What is next to   ?  

What is up in the air? 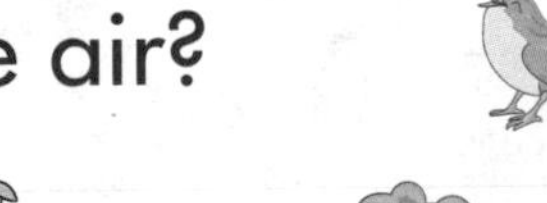 

What is near  ?  

What is above  ?  

What is far from  ?  

What is beside  ? 

What is down on the ground?  

NAME ____________________

Check What You Learned

Geometry

Write the name of each shape.

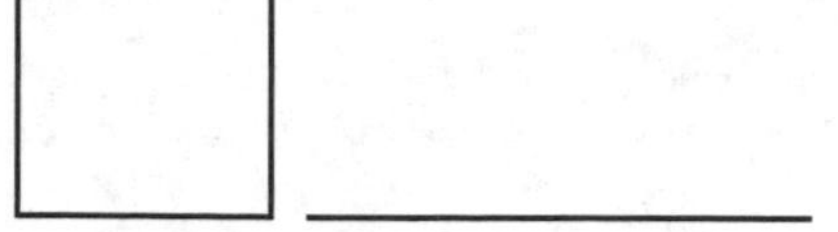 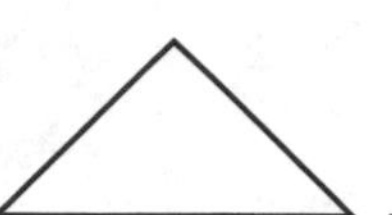 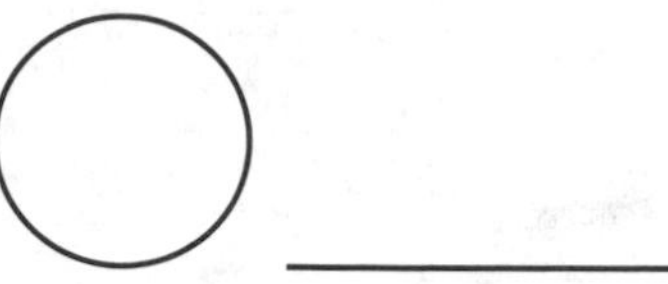

Write the letter R on the rectangles. Write the letter T on the triangles, C on circles, and S on squares.

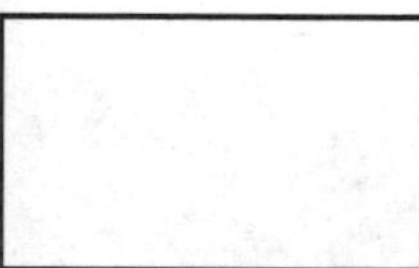 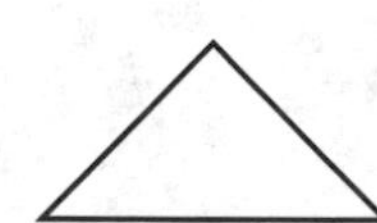  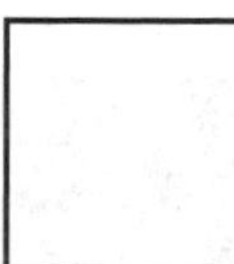 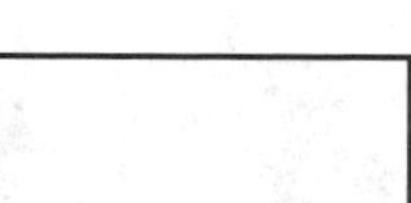 

Write the name of each shape. Then, draw the shape.

____

____

____

Check What You Know

Preparing for Algebra

How many?

Write the number and the number word.

Look at each picture. Write if it is a *slide*, *flip*, or *turn*.

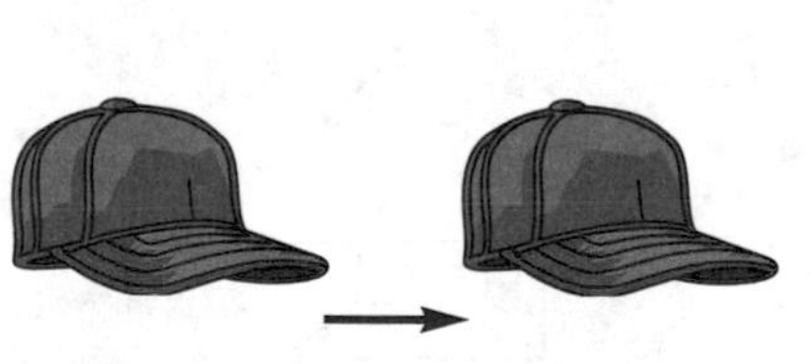

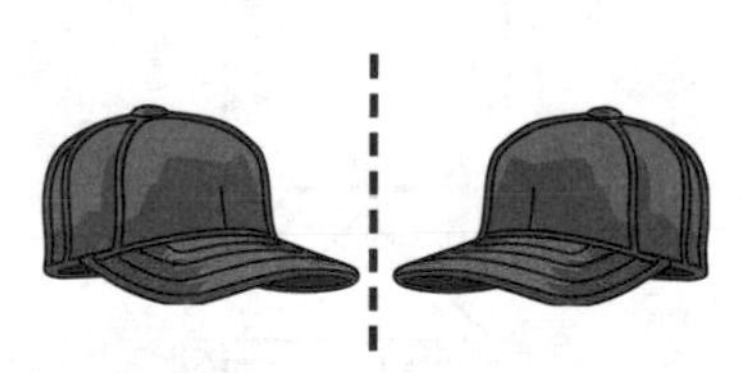

NAME ____________________

Check What You Know

Preparing for Algebra

Find the pattern. Write the next 2 numbers.

3, 4, 3, 5, 3, 4, 3, 5, 3, 4, ____, ____

9, 8, 7, 9, 8, 7, 9, 8, 7, 9, ____, ____

2, 4, 6, 8, 2, 4, 6, 8, 2, 4, ____, ____

Start with the arrow. Find the pattern.
Draw the shape that comes next.

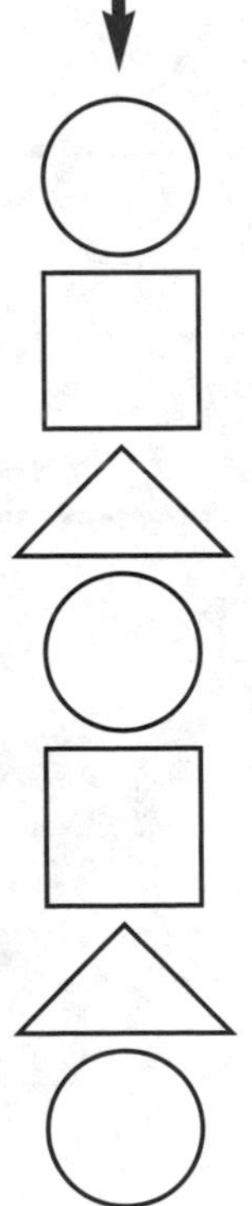

____

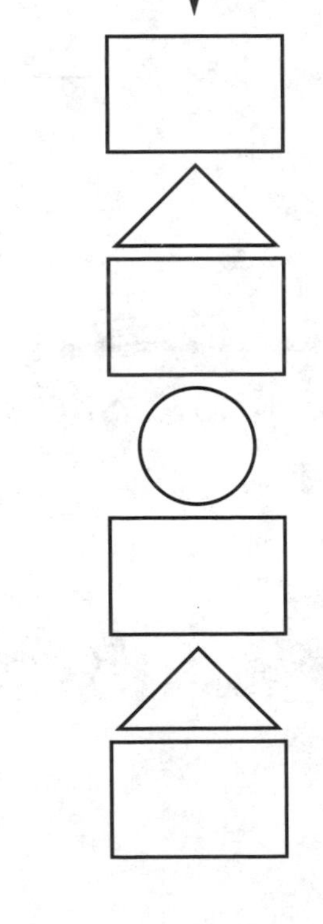

____

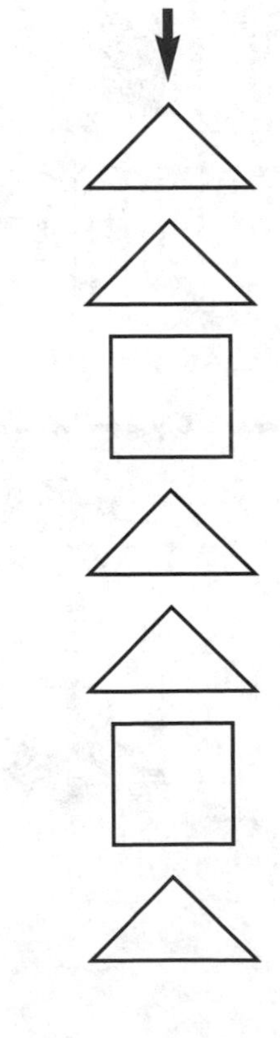

____

NAME ____________________

Lesson 8.1 Sorting and Classifying Objects

2
two

3
three

How many? Write the number and the number word.

3 ____ three ____________

____ ____________

____ ____________

____ ____________

____ ____________

____ ____________

____ ____________

____ ____________

____ ____________

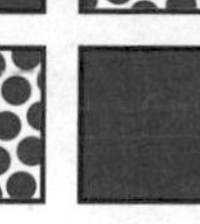

____ ____________

____ ____________

NAME ___________________________

Lesson 8.1 Sorting and Classifying Objects

How many? Write the number and the number word.

3 three

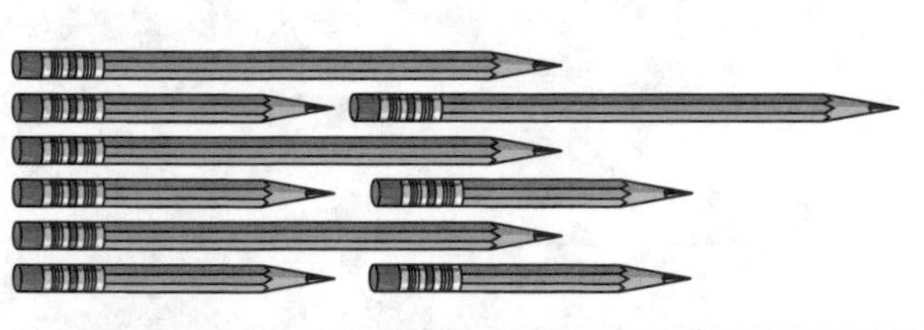

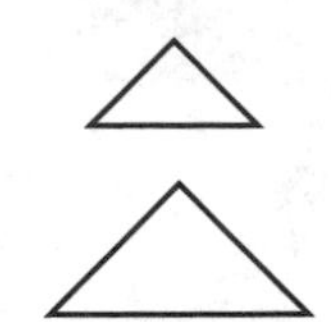

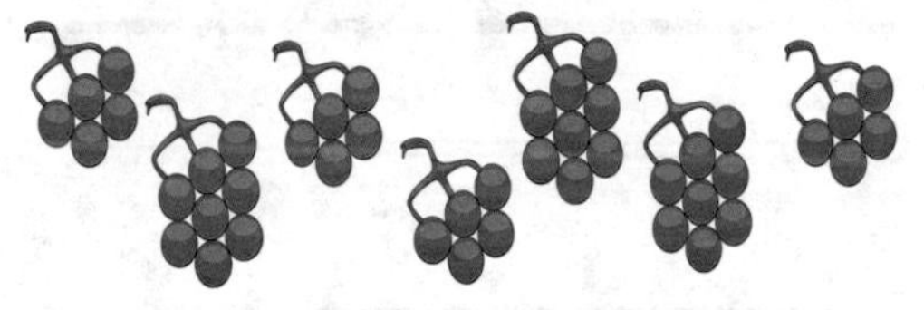

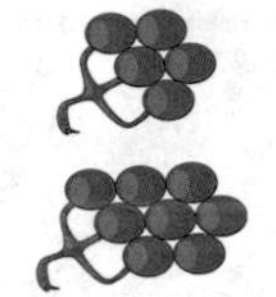

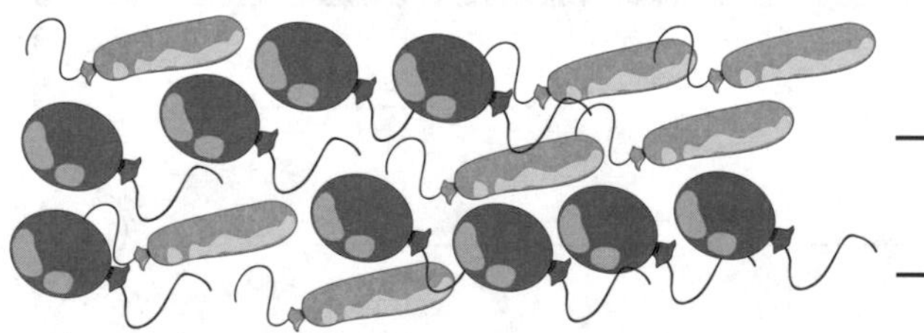

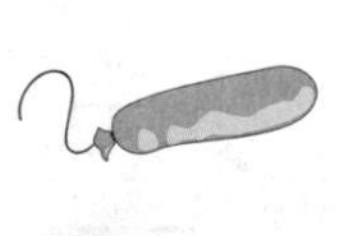

NAME ______________________

Lesson 8.2 Number Patterns

Find the pattern. Write the missing numbers.

2, 4, 6, 8, 2, 4, 6, 8, 2, 4, __6__, __8__

1, 2, 3, 1, 2, 3, 1, 2, 3, 1, 2, 3, 1, ____, ____

1, 2, 1, 3, ____, ____, 1, 2, 1, 3, 1, 4

6, 5, 4, 3, 6, 5, 4, 3, 6, 5, ____, ____

6, 8, ____, ____, 6, 8, 6, 10, 6, 8, 6, 10

2, 3, 5, 2, 3, 5, 2, 3, 5, 2, ____, ____

8, 6, 4, 8, 6, 4, 8, 6, 4, 8, ____, ____

10, 9, ____, ____, 10, 9, 8, 7, 10, 9, 8, 7

4, 5, 6, 7, 8, 4, 5, 6, 7, 8, ____, ____

____, ____, 10, 5, 10, 5, 10, 5, 10, 5, 10, 5

8, 7, 8, 6, 8, 7, 8, 6, 8, 7, ____, ____

5, 6, 7, 5, 6, 7, 5, 6, 7, 5, ____, ____

NAME ______________________

Lesson 8.3 Geometric Patterns

Start with the arrow. Find the pattern.

Draw the shape that comes next.

Lesson 8.4 Flips, Slides, and Turns

slide

flip

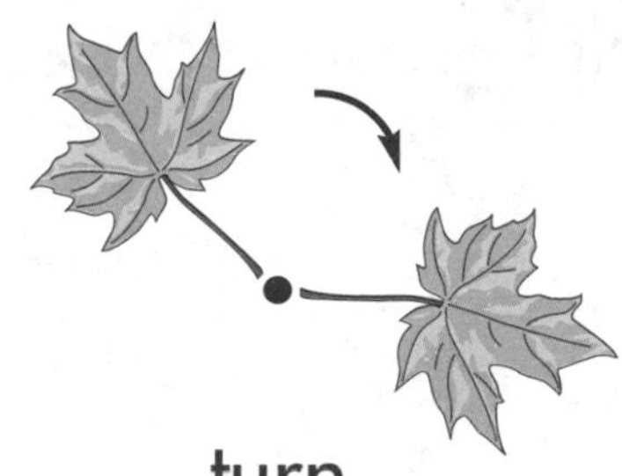

turn

Tell if each pictures is a *slide*, *flip*, or *turn*.

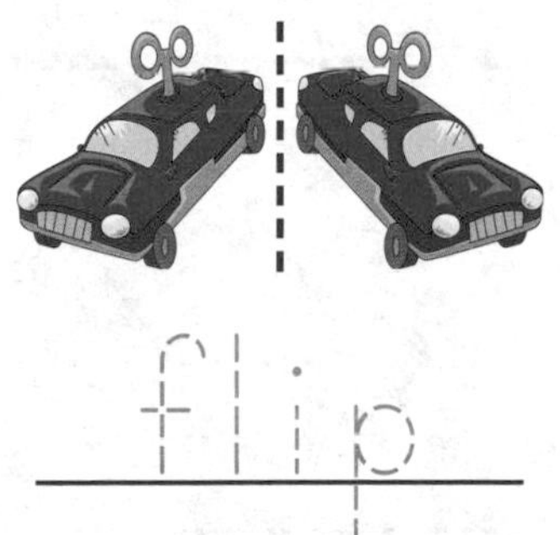	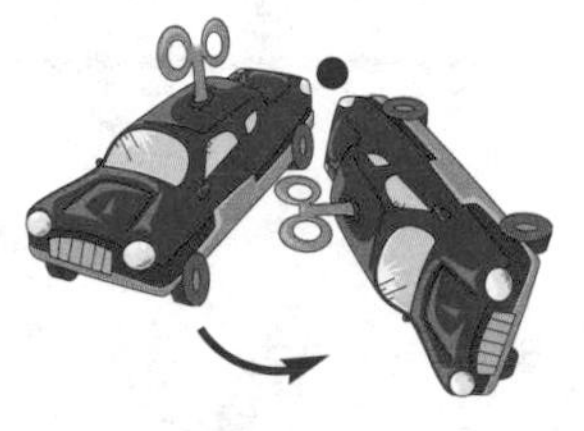 ________	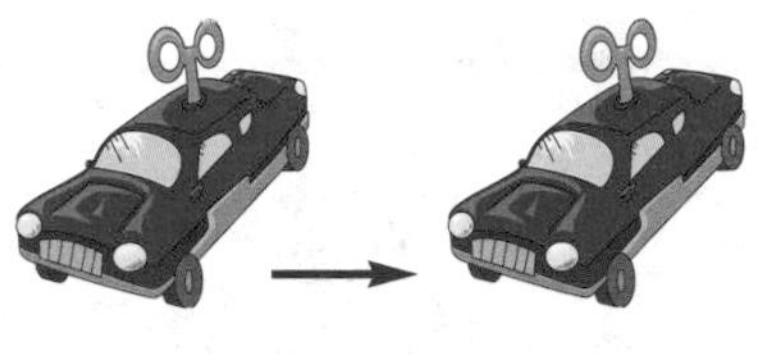 ________
 ________	 ________	 ________
 ________	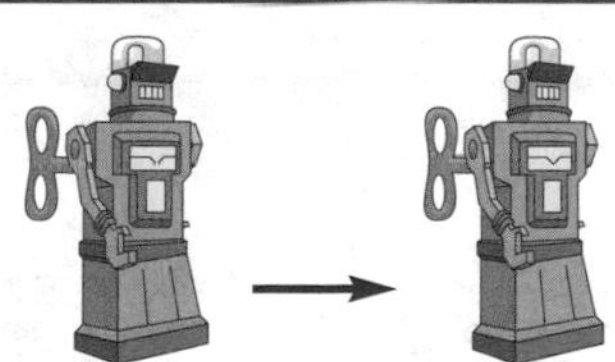 ________	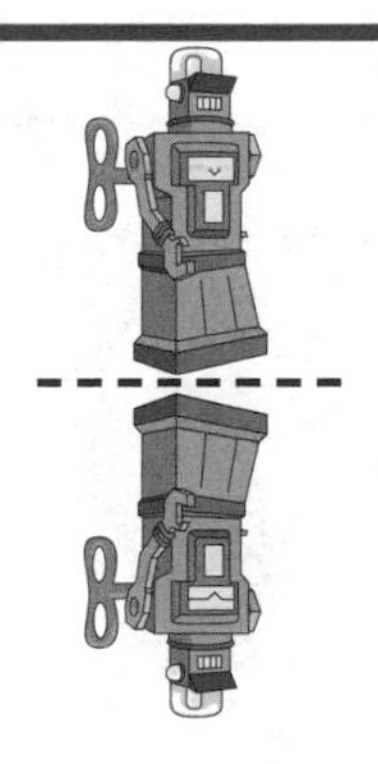 ________

NAME ______________________

Lesson 8.4 Flips, Slides, and Turns

Tell if each pictures is a *slide*, *flip*, or *turn*.

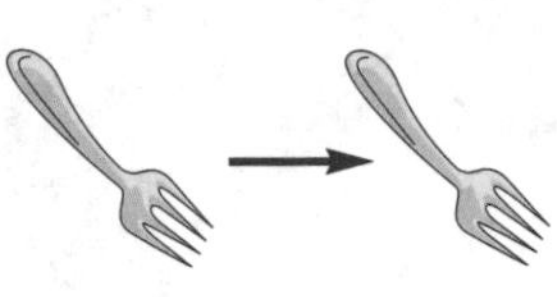 slide	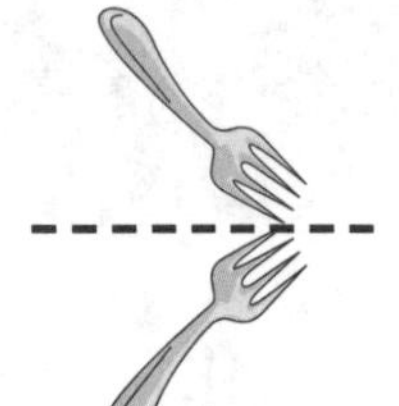 ______	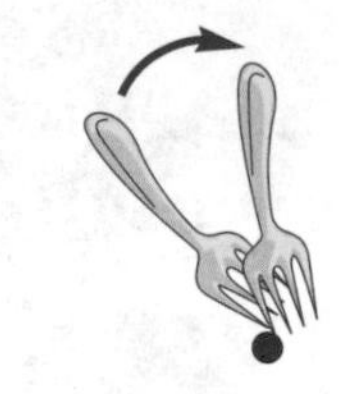 ______
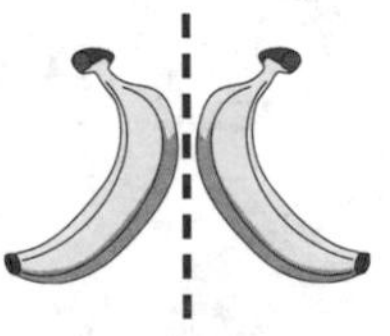 ______	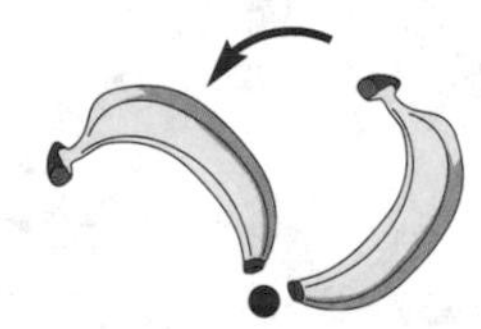 ______	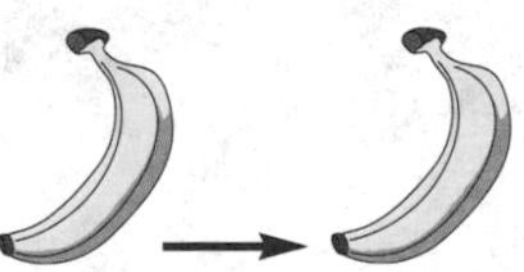 ______
 ______	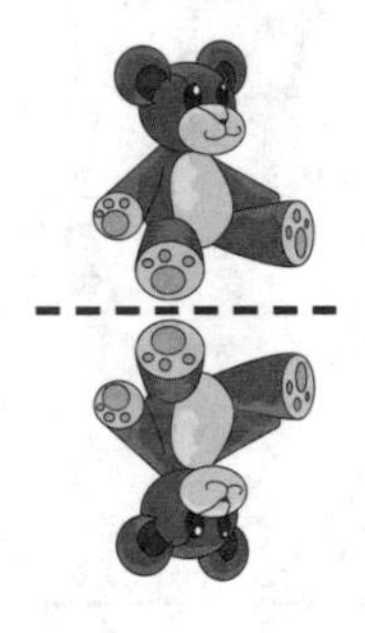 ______	 ______
 ______	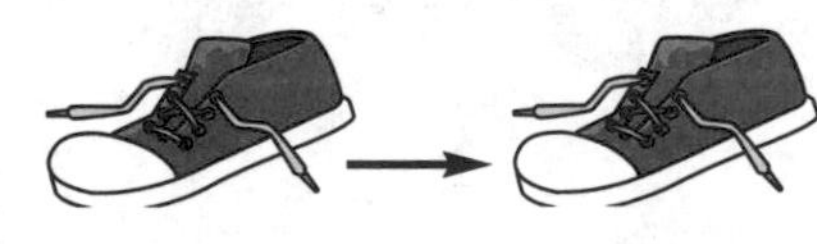 ______	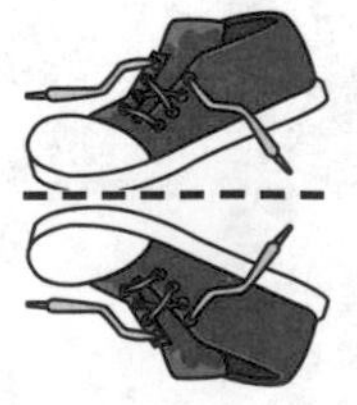 ______

NAME ______________________

Check What You Learned

Preparing for Algebra

How many? Write the number and the number word.

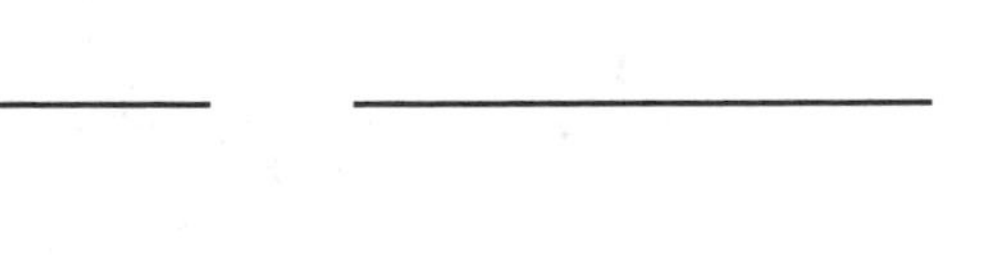

CHAPTER 8 POSTTEST

Look at each picture. Write if it is a *slide, flip,* or *turn*.

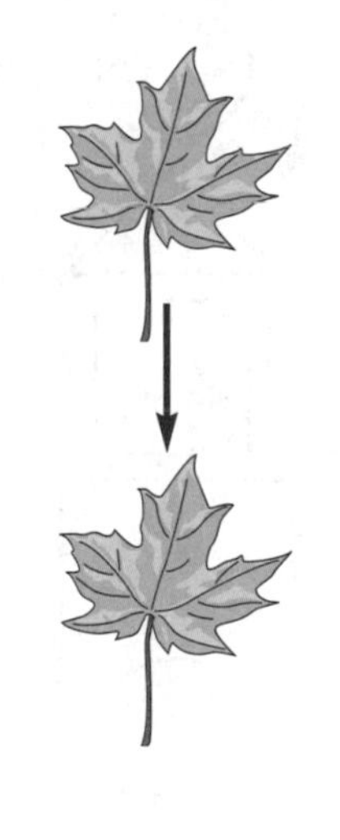

____

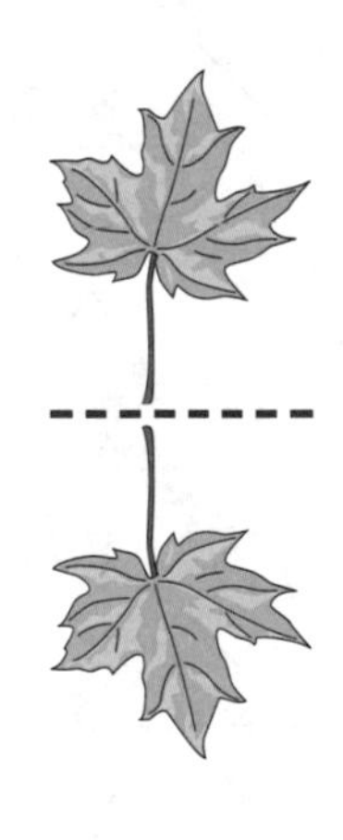

____

____

NAME ______________________

Check What You Learned

Preparing for Algebra

Find the pattern. Write the missing numbers.

10, 6, 8, 10, 6, 8, 10, 6, 8, 10, ____, ____

4, ____, ____, 4, 5, 6, 4, 5, 6, 4, 5, 6

4, 3, 2, 1, 4, 3, ____, ____, 4, 3, 2, 1

Start with the arrow. Find the pattern.

Draw the shape that comes next.

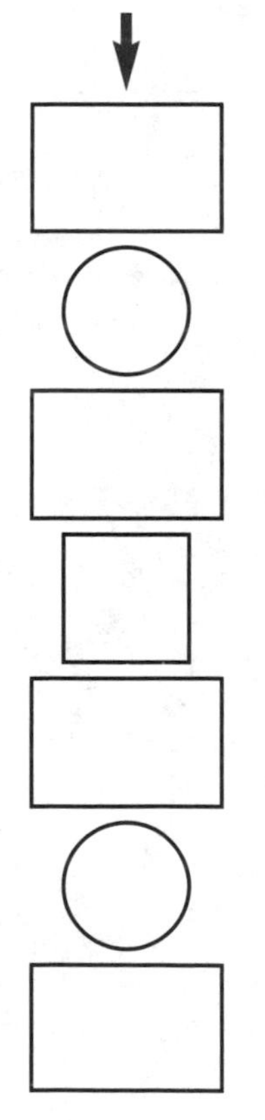

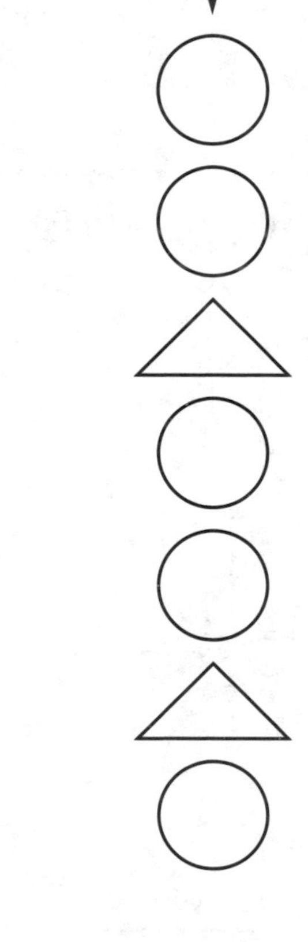

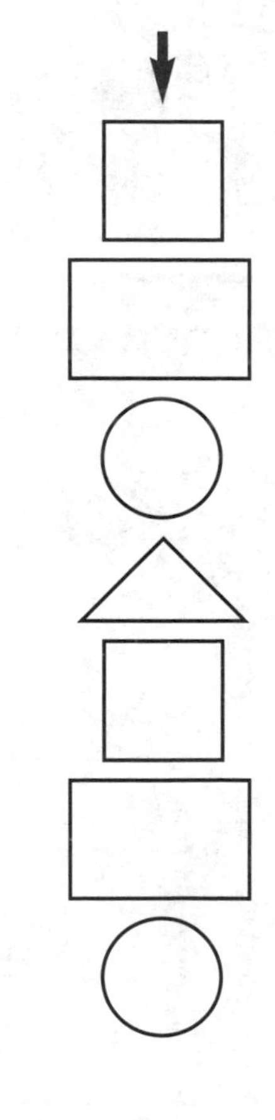

CHAPTER 8 POSTTEST

NAME ______________________

Final Test Chapters 1–8

Add.

5 +3	8 +4	9 +2	6 +4	7 +1	3 +2
7 +8	8 +9	4 +1	4 +5	8 +8	2 +1
4 +3	6 +8	7 +5	3 +3	1 +3	9 +0
0 +1	9 +9	7 +7	6 +7	1 +1	2 +5
5 +5	7 +0	1 +9	9 +8	6 +9	0 +0
6 +3	2 +2	8 +2	9 +7	4 +4	9 +5
6 +6	8 +5	1 +5	5 +0	6 +1	0 +8

NAME ____________________

Final Test Chapters 1–8

Subtract.

$\begin{array}{r}18\\-9\\\hline\end{array}$	$\begin{array}{r}12\\-4\\\hline\end{array}$	$\begin{array}{r}11\\-2\\\hline\end{array}$	$\begin{array}{r}10\\-4\\\hline\end{array}$	$\begin{array}{r}8\\-7\\\hline\end{array}$	$\begin{array}{r}5\\-2\\\hline\end{array}$
$\begin{array}{r}15\\-8\\\hline\end{array}$	$\begin{array}{r}17\\-9\\\hline\end{array}$	$\begin{array}{r}9\\-7\\\hline\end{array}$	$\begin{array}{r}7\\-3\\\hline\end{array}$	$\begin{array}{r}13\\-5\\\hline\end{array}$	$\begin{array}{r}3\\-1\\\hline\end{array}$
$\begin{array}{r}9\\-5\\\hline\end{array}$	$\begin{array}{r}14\\-8\\\hline\end{array}$	$\begin{array}{r}12\\-5\\\hline\end{array}$	$\begin{array}{r}6\\-3\\\hline\end{array}$	$\begin{array}{r}4\\-3\\\hline\end{array}$	$\begin{array}{r}9\\-0\\\hline\end{array}$
$\begin{array}{r}1\\-1\\\hline\end{array}$	$\begin{array}{r}15\\-6\\\hline\end{array}$	$\begin{array}{r}14\\-7\\\hline\end{array}$	$\begin{array}{r}13\\-7\\\hline\end{array}$	$\begin{array}{r}2\\-1\\\hline\end{array}$	$\begin{array}{r}7\\-5\\\hline\end{array}$
$\begin{array}{r}15\\-9\\\hline\end{array}$	$\begin{array}{r}7\\-0\\\hline\end{array}$	$\begin{array}{r}10\\-9\\\hline\end{array}$	$\begin{array}{r}17\\-8\\\hline\end{array}$	$\begin{array}{r}5\\-5\\\hline\end{array}$	$\begin{array}{r}3\\-0\\\hline\end{array}$
$\begin{array}{r}6\\-3\\\hline\end{array}$	$\begin{array}{r}4\\-2\\\hline\end{array}$	$\begin{array}{r}10\\-2\\\hline\end{array}$	$\begin{array}{r}5\\-1\\\hline\end{array}$	$\begin{array}{r}8\\-4\\\hline\end{array}$	$\begin{array}{r}14\\-5\\\hline\end{array}$
$\begin{array}{r}12\\-6\\\hline\end{array}$	$\begin{array}{r}16\\-8\\\hline\end{array}$	$\begin{array}{r}6\\-5\\\hline\end{array}$	$\begin{array}{r}5\\-0\\\hline\end{array}$	$\begin{array}{r}7\\-1\\\hline\end{array}$	$\begin{array}{r}8\\-8\\\hline\end{array}$

NAME ___________________

Final Test Chapters 1–8

SHOW YOUR WORK

Solve each problem.

I have .

I find .

How much money do I have? ________¢

There are 7  .

4 more  come.

How many  are there in all? ________

There are 8 .

There are 2 .

What is 8 plus 2? ________

Joseph buys  for 7¢.

He buys 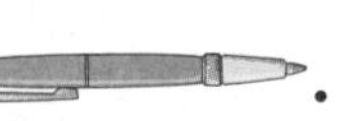 for 9¢.

How much money did he spend? ________¢

Imala has 5  .

She has 3 .

What is 5 plus 3? ________

There are 6 hippos.

6 more come.

What is 6 + 6? ________

CHAPTERS 1–8 FINAL TEST

NAME ______________________

Final Test Chapters 1–8

Solve each problem.

Pamela has .
She buys [pen] for 8¢.
How much money does she have left? ________¢

There are 17 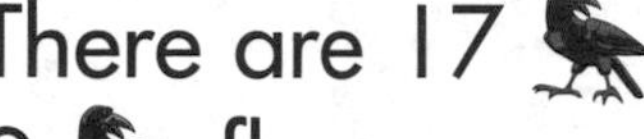.
9 fly away.
What is 17 minus 9? ________

Myron wants 18 .
He has 9 .
How many more  does he want? ________

Omar has 14 .
Lulu has 1 .
How much more money does Omar have? ________¢

There are 7 .
3  run away.
How many  are left? ________

Kiru has 15 .
She gives 6 away.
How many does she have left? ________

NAME ____________________

Final Test Chapters 1–8

Count and write how much money.

______ ¢

______ ¢

______ ¢

______ ¢

______ ¢

______ ¢

______ ¢

______ ¢

______ ¢

______ ¢

NAME ________________________________

Final Test Chapters 1–8

Look at the picture graph.

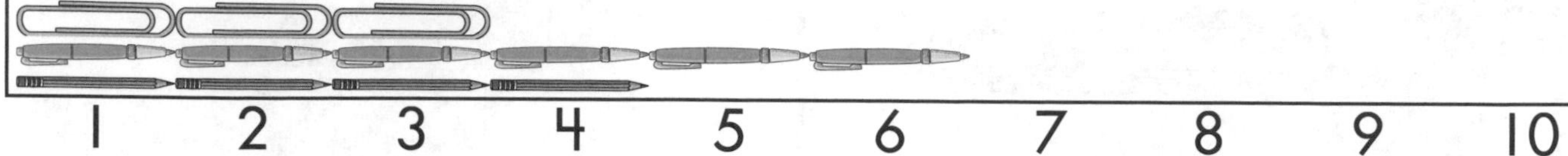

Circle your answer.

Which is more?

Which is fewer?

Complete.

How many ? ________

How many ? ________

How many ? ________

Circle your answer.

What is next to ?  

What is below ?  

What is up on the top shelf?  

What is down on the bottom shelf?  

What is above ?  

What is beside ?  

NAME ______________________________ DATE ______________

Scoring Record for Posttests, Mid-Test, and Final Test

		Performance			
Chapter Posttest	Your Score	Excellent	Very Good	Fair	Needs Improvement
1	___ of 17	17	15–16	11–14	10 or fewer
2	___ of 42	40–42	35–39	26–34	25 or fewer
3	___ of 42	40–42	35–39	26–34	25 or fewer
4	___ of 48	46–48	39–45	30–38	29 or fewer
5	___ of 41	39–41	34–38	26–33	25 or fewer
6	___ of 22	21–22	19–20	14–18	13 or fewer
7	___ of 19	19	16–18	12–15	11 or fewer
8	___ of 20	20	17–19	13–16	12 or fewer
Mid-Test	___ of 136	127–136	110–126	83–109	82 or fewer
Final Test	___ of 117	110–117	95–109	71–94	70 or fewer

Record your test score in the Your Score column. See where your score falls in the Performance columns. Your score is based on the total number of required responses. If your score is fair or needs improvement, review the chapter material.

Grade 1 Answers

Chapter 1

Lesson 1.1, page 1

0	1	2	(3)	4	0	1	2	3	(4)
(0)	1	2	3	4	0	(1)	2	3	4
0	1	(2)	3	4	0	1	2	(3)	4

Lesson 1.2, page 2

(5)	6	7	5	6	(7)
5	6	(7)	5	(6)	7
5	(6)	7	(5)	6	7

Lesson 1.3, page 3

8	(9)	10	(8)	9	10
8	(9)	10	8	9	(10)
(8)	9	10	8	9	(10)

Lesson 1.4, page 4

0
1
2
3
4
5
6
7
8
9
10

Lesson 1.5, page 5

six	four
two	seven
five	ten
eight	three

Lesson 1.5, page 6

8	4
5	9
10	7
3	1

Lesson 1.6, page 7

1	2	3	4	5
6	7	8	9	10
10	9	8	7	6
5	4	3	2	1
1	2	3	4	5
6	7	8	9	10

Lesson 1.6, page 8

2	4	6	8	10
3	4	5	6	7
10	8	6	4	2
9	8	7	6	5
0	2	4	6	8
7	6	5	4	3
5	6	7	8	9

Lesson 1.7, page 9

Lesson 1.7, page 10

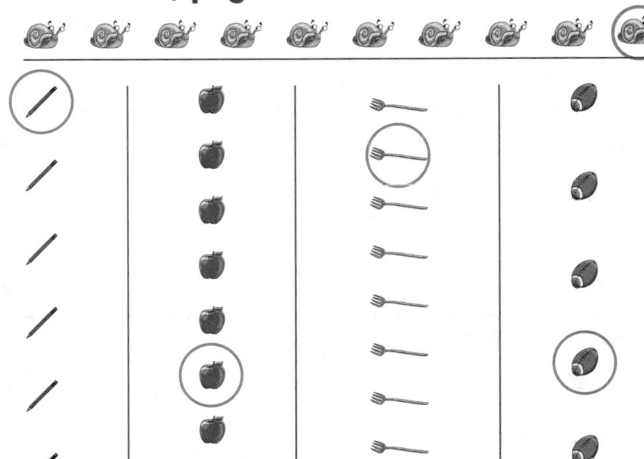

Grade 1 Answers

Lesson 1.8, page 11

4¢	6¢
3¢	7¢
5¢	2¢
5¢	4¢

Lesson 1.8, page 12

8¢	10¢
7¢	6¢
10¢	9¢
8¢	10¢

Posttest, page 13

six	three	eight		
2	7	9		
2	3	4	5	6
7	6	5	4	3
8	6	4	2	0

Posttest, page 14

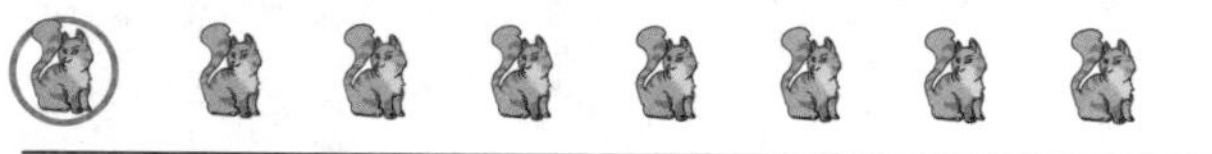

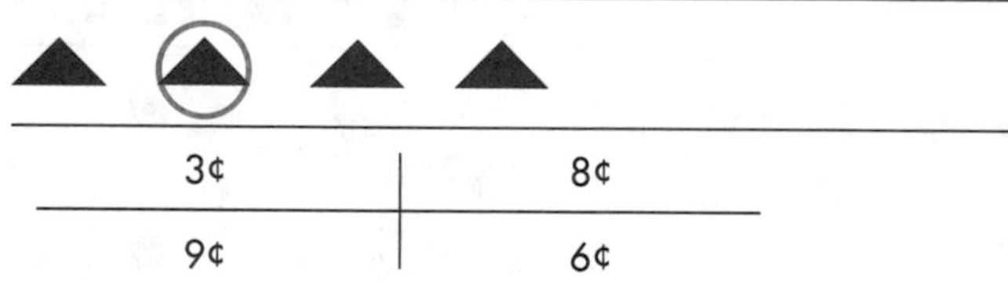

3¢	8¢
9¢	6¢

Chapter 2

Pretest, page 15

6	5	2	6	6	5
4	3	3	4	6	3
6	6	4			
4	6	6			
5	2	2	2	2	3
3	2	1	1	1	5
1	4	1			
3	1	0			

Pretest, page 16

6
3
2
3

Lesson 2.1, page 17

2 2	3 3 3 3
1 1 1 1	2 2 2 2
3 3 3 3	0 0

Lesson 2.2, page 18

1 1	0 0
2 2	1 1
2 2	0 0
0 0	1 1

Lesson 2.3, page 19

5 5 5 5	4 4
4 4 4 4	5 5 5 5
4 4 4 4	5 5 5 5

Grade 1 Answers

Lesson 2.4, page 20

3 3	0 0
2 2	4 4
5 5	3 3
1 1	1 1

Lesson 2.5, page 21

6 6 6 6	6 6 6 6
6 6 6 6	6 6

6 6 5 6 6 5
5 6 6
6 6 4

Lesson 2.6, page 22

2 2	5 5
6 6	3 3
4 4	1 1

5 3 4 0 2 1

Lesson 2.7, page 23

5 5 3 2	6 6 1 5
4 4 1 3	6 3
3 3 2 1	4 4 0 4
4 2	5 5 1 4

Lesson 2.8, page 24

3
4
2
3
5
5

Lesson 2.8, page 25

6
6
6
2
2
4

Lesson 2.8, page 26

2
5
1
1
4
2

Posttest, page 27

5	6	5	6	3	4
6	4	4	1	6	5
4	3	5	2	6	6
3	5	0	3	1	6
2	2	2	3	0	1
3	1	4	1	4	0

Posttest, page 28

5
3
3
6
1
4

Chapter 3

Pretest, page 29

10	9	10	8	8	7
8	9	9	10	10	7
10	5	7	9	10	8
5	2	6	2	6	9
1	7	0	4	7	3
9	1	4	8	7	1

Grade 1 Answers

Pretest, page 30

9
3
3¢
7
5
10¢

Lesson 3.1, page 31

7	7
7	7
7	7
7	7
7	7
7	7
7	7
7	7

7 7 6 7 7 7

Lesson 3.2, page 32

4	6
4	6
2	7
2	7
1	3
1	3
5	0
5	0

Lesson 3.3, page 33

8	8
8	8
8	8
8	8
8	8
8	8
8	
8	

7 8 8 8 7 8

Lesson 3.4, page 34

6	4
6	4
2	1
2	1
7	0
7	0
5	3
5	3

Lesson 3.5, page 35

9	9
9	9
9	9
9	9
9	9
9	9
9	9
9	9
9	9
9	9

9 9 9 9 9 9

Lesson 3.6, page 36

2	6
2	6
4	8
4	8
7	5
7	5

3 0 9 1

Lesson 3.7, page 37

10	10
10	10
10	10
10	10
10	10
10	10
10	10
10	10

10 10 10 10 10 10

Grade 1 Answers

Lesson 3.8, page 38

4 4	5 5
7 7	2 2
9 9	0 0
8 8	1 1
3 3	6 6

Lesson 3.9, page 39

8	9	9	10	8	7
9	7	10	10	9	10
8	10	7	8	10	9
7	7	10	10	7	9
9	10	7	3	10	8
9	6	7	9	10	3

Lesson 3.9, page 40

10
9
8
7
10

Lesson 3.10, page 41

6	1	6	4	9	0
2	8	4	3	4	0
3	0	5	3	8	7
5	1	0	6	4	10
5	1	7	7	9	2
2	2	3	7	4	3

Lesson 3.10, page 42

3
7
4
5
4

Lesson 3.11, page 43

7¢	10¢
8¢	9¢
10¢	5¢
8¢	6¢

Lesson 3.12, page 44

7¢
10¢
8¢
5¢
1¢
9¢

Lesson 3.13, page 45

9	9	5	4	10	10	7	3
			7 7 2 5				9 9 3 6
8	8	7	1	10	5		
7	7	3	4	8	8	6	2

Lesson 3.14, page 46

9
9
8
8
8
6
9
10
7

Lesson 3.15, page 47

4	4
7	7
5	5
6	6
4	4
6	6
2	2
1	1
3	3

Lesson 3.16, page 48

	4	6	7
2	3		10
6		8	9
8			2
4	5	6	7

Grade 1 Answers

Posttest, page 49

9	7	8	10	10	9
9	10	8	7	8	10
9	8	7	10	8	7
2	10	4	4	0	3
8	8	5	3	5	5
1	0	3	8	6	7

Posttest, page 50

6
10¢
8
7
2¢
8¢

Chapter 4

Pretest, page 51

3 tens 6 ones = 36
5 tens 2 ones = 52
4 tens 1 one = 41
1 ten 2 ones = 12

96	78
84	49
63	16
57	34
20	81

Pretest, page 52

25	28	30	31
36	44	46	52
84	76	70	68
20	40	45	60
75	60	50	35
30	50	60	90

5 | 40

Lesson 4.1, page 53

1 ten 0 ones = 10
1 ten 0 ones = 10
1 ten 1 one = 11
1 ten 1 one = 11
1 ten 2 ones = 12
1 ten 2 ones = 12
1 ten 3 ones = 13
1 ten 3 ones = 13
1 ten 4 ones = 14
1 ten 4 ones = 14

Lesson 4.2, page 54

1 ten 5 ones = 15
1 ten 5 ones = 15
1 ten 6 ones = 16
1 ten 6 ones = 16
1 ten 7 ones = 17
1 ten 7 ones = 17
1 ten 8 ones = 18
1 ten 8 ones = 18
1 ten 9 ones = 19
1 ten 9 ones = 19

Lesson 4.3, page 55

2 tens 0 ones = 20
2 tens 0 ones = 20
2 tens 1 one = 21
2 tens 1 one = 21
2 tens 2 ones = 22
2 tens 2 ones = 22
2 tens 3 ones = 23
2 tens 3 ones = 23
2 tens 4 ones = 24
2 tens 4 ones = 24

Lesson 4.4, page 56

2 tens 5 ones = 25
2 tens 5 ones = 25
2 tens 6 ones = 26
2 tens 6 ones = 26
2 tens 7 ones = 27
2 tens 7 ones = 27
2 tens 8 ones = 28
2 tens 8 ones = 28
2 tens 9 ones = 29
2 tens 9 ones = 29

Lesson 4.5, page 57

3 tens 4 ones = 34
4 tens 2 ones = 42
3 tens 0 ones = 30
4 tens 3 ones = 43

44	39
36	45
41	37
38	40
46	33

Lesson 4.6, page 58

5 tens 1 one = 51
6 tens 3 ones = 63
5 tens 4 ones = 54
6 tens 2 ones = 62

60	69
52	64
67	55
53	66
58	57

Lesson 4.7, page 59

76	98
83	80
71	75
87	99
94	91
92	86
79	70
88	82

Lesson 4.8, page 60

38	40	43	46
46	52	58	60
26	32	38	46
30	45	55	70
5	20	40	60
10	40	60	90
78	75	71	68
82	76	68	66
20	14	10	4
90	75	60	55
65	50	30	20
80	50	40	20

Lesson 4.9, page 61

5	90
90	40
40	5

Lesson 4.10, page 62

3¢
8¢
10¢
8¢
0¢
7¢

Posttest, page 63

2 tens 4 ones = 24
3 tens 3 ones = 33
6 tens 0 ones = 60
1 ten 5 ones = 15

48	81
73	58
95	39
62	27
56	11

Posttest, page 64

49	52	53	56
24	30	38	40
66	60	54	48
20	35	50	65
55	40	30	10
10	30	70	90

90	5

Mid-Test

page 65

7	3
2	10

3 tens 6 ones = 36	5 tens 5 ones = 55
4 tens 0 ones = 40	9 tens 7 ones = 97

page 66

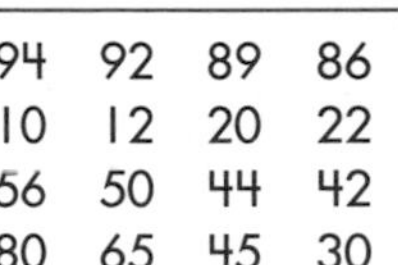

94	92	89	86
10	12	20	22
56	50	44	42
80	65	45	30
20	30	60	80

Grade 1 Answers

page 67

9	5	9	8	9	10
9	7	10	5	6	4
10	9	6	7	8	5
1	6	7	10	8	7
10	6	8	5	8	2
0	3	6	5	4	7
8	8	10	9	9	10

page 68

2	1	8	3	2	2
3	1	4	0	2	1
6	2	0	1	4	6
6	3	3	3	0	7
5	0	8	8	2	9
2	3	0	2	0	5
5	10	7	4	1	0

page 69

9¢
8
6
5¢
10¢
5

page 70

4¢
2
5
2¢
6
1¢

Chapter 5

Pretest, page 71

11	18	15	14	13	12
17	16	16	13	12	11
15	13	14	17	16	15
8	4	9	9	6	7
7	7	9	9	8	6
3	8	8	7	7	6

Pretest, page 72

17
7
7
14
7

Lesson 5.1, page 73

11	11
11	11
11	11
11	11

11 11 11 11 11 11

Lesson 5.2, page 74

3	8
6	2
7	4
9	5

8 5 2 3 7 11

Lesson 5.3, page 75

12	12
12	12
12	12

12 12 12 12 12 12
12 12 12
12 12 12

Lesson 5.4, page 76

5	7
6	3
4	9

8 9 4 5 6 7
3 4 6
5 9 8

Lesson 5.5, page 77

13	13
13	13
13	13

13 13 13 13 13 13
13 13 13
13 13 13

Lesson 5.6, page 78

4	9
7	8
5	13

4 5 8 6 13 7
6 5 9
8 4 7

Grade 1 Answers

Lesson 5.7, page 79

14	14
14	14
14	14

14 14 14 14 14 14
13 14 14

Lesson 5.8, page 80

8	6
9	14
7	5

14 7 6 5 8 9
7 5 8
6 12 11

Lesson 5.9, page 81

11 13 12 14 12 11
13 13 11 12 11 12
14 12 11 13 12 14
5 9 8 5 5 6
9 7 8 4 3 7
9 7 7 4 6 3

Lesson 5.9, page 82

6
14
4
13
5
12

Lesson 5.10, page 83

15 15
15 14 15 13 14 13
15 13 15 14 14 13
6 9
6 7 9 5 8 6
8 9 9 4 7 6

Lesson 5.10, page 84

6
15
15
8
9

Lesson 5.11, page 85

16 16
14 16 15 16 14 15
15 14 16 14 14 15
7 9
8 8 5 6 7 9
9 6 7 9 7 8

Lesson 5.11, page 86

16
8
9
16
16

Lesson 5.12, page 87

17 18
16 17 14 15 18 14
15 14 17 15 16 15
8 9 9
7 8 7 9 9 9
9 8 7 8 8 9

Lesson 5.12, page 88

8
18
17
9
9

Lesson 5.13, page 89

17 16 15 15 13 14
18 16 15 17 14 13
13 14 15 16 14 13
5 8 8 7 7 8
9 9 6 9 9 9
7 5 7 6 9 6

Lesson 5.13, page 90

8
15
9
16
9

Posttest, page 91

15 17 13 11 11 14
12 13 16 12 12 18
12 15 13 11 15 14
9 8 5 8 7 8
9 7 6 8 4 9
4 7 9 8 4 6

Posttest, page 92

6
13
9
15
16

Grade 1 Answers

Chapter 6

Pretest, page 93

25¢	13¢
12¢	15¢

4:00	3:30	10:30
4 o'clock	3 thirty	10 thirty

Monday
4
Monday
Saturday
Thursday

Pretest, page 94

4
3

Lesson 6.1, page 95

25¢	5¢
60¢	23¢
10¢	15¢
10¢	80¢

Lesson 6.1, page 96

76¢	31¢
43¢	45¢
30¢	60¢
52¢	26¢

Lesson 6.2, page 97

4:00 4 o'clock	9:00 9 o'clock
3:00 3 o'clock	7:00 7 o'clock
12:00 12 o'clock	2:00 2 o'clock
1:00 1 o'clock	6:00 6 o'clock

Lesson 6.2, page 98

6:00	7:00
8:00	2:00

Lesson 6.3, page 99

1:30 1 thirty	5:30 5 thirty
7:30 7 thirty	10:30 10 thirty
12:30 12 thirty	2:30 2 thirty
6:30 6 thirty	9:30 9 thirty

Lesson 6.3, page 100

4:30	11:30
8:30	3:30

Lesson 6.4, page 101

Wednesday
Sunday
Friday
4
Wednesday, June 30
Monday
Wednesday
Saturday

Grade 1 Answers

Lesson 6.4, page 102

January
May
February
4
7
December
September
April

Lesson 6.5, page 103

7	8
4	5
6	
5	

Lesson 6.5, page 104

5	5
3	4
6	

Lesson 6.6, page 105

4
7
12
9

Lesson 6.7, page 106

12
6
the bowl

Lesson 6.8, page 107

6
8
4
7
10

Lesson 6.9, page 108

less than
greater than
equal to
greater than

Lesson 6.10, page 109

Answers will vary.

Lesson 6.10, page 110

Answers will vary.

Posttest, page 111

30¢	11¢
22¢	25¢

9:30	7:30	2:00
9 thirty	7 thirty	2 o'clock

Sunday
Wednesday
Friday, August 31
Sunday
4

Posttest, page 112

4
6

 | 

equal to
greater than
less than

Grade 1 Answers

Chapter 7

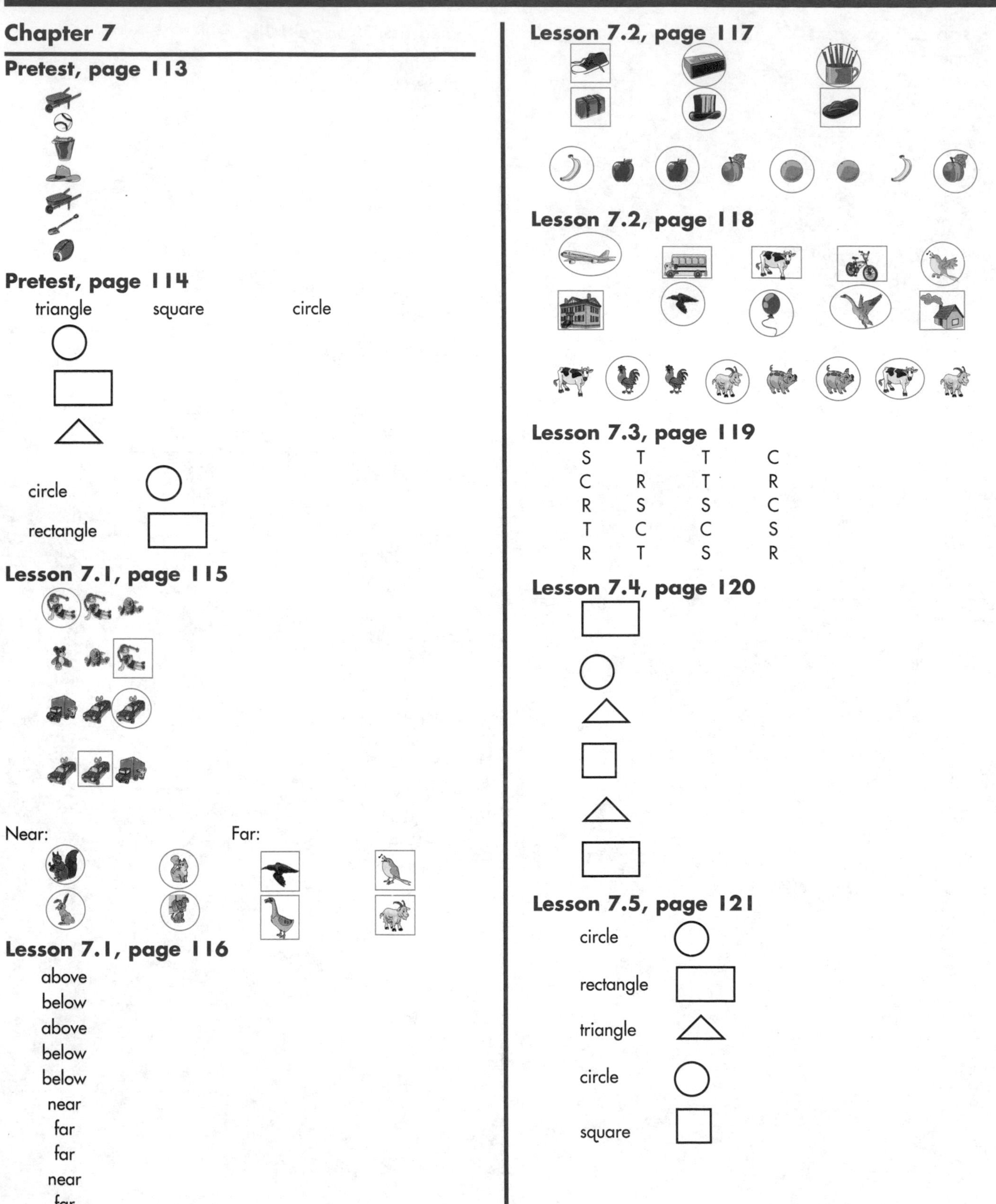

Pretest, page 113

Pretest, page 114

triangle square circle

circle

rectangle

Lesson 7.1, page 115

Near:

Far:

Lesson 7.1, page 116

above
below
above
below
below
near
far
far
near
far

Lesson 7.2, page 117

Lesson 7.2, page 118

Lesson 7.3, page 119

S	T	T	C
C	R	T	R
R	S	S	C
T	C	C	S
R	T	S	R

Lesson 7.4, page 120

Lesson 7.5, page 121

circle

rectangle

triangle

circle

square

Grade 1 Answers

Lesson 7.5, page 122

triangle △ 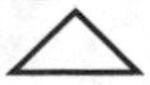
square □ 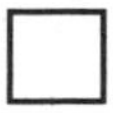
rectangle ▭ 
triangle △ 
circle ○

Posttest, page 123

Posttest, page 124

square triangle circle
R T C S R T

square □ 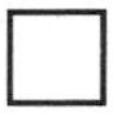
circle ○ 
triangle △

Chapter 8

Pretest, page 125

2 two
4 four
3 three
5 five
slide flip turn

Pretest, page 126

3, 5
8, 7
6, 8
□ ○ △

Lesson 8.1, page 127

3 three
4 four

6 six
2 two

3 three
5 five

6 six
3 three
4 four

4 four
5 five

Lesson 8.1, page 128

3 three
2 two
5 five

5 five
7 seven

4 four
5 five

4 four
3 three

7 seven
9 nine

6 six
5 five

Lesson 8.2, page 129

6, 8
2, 3
1, 4
4, 3
6, 10
3, 5
6, 4
8, 7
4, 5
10, 5
8, 6
6, 7

Grade 1 Answers

Lesson 8.3, page 130

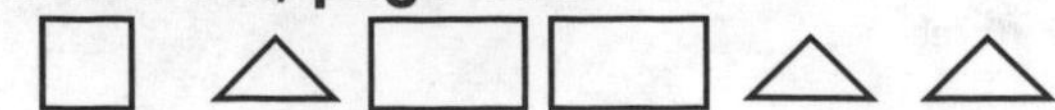

Lesson 8.4, page 131

flip	turn	slide
slide	flip	turn
turn	slide	flip

Lesson 8.4, page 132

slide	flip	turn
flip	turn	slide
slide	flip	turn
turn	slide	flip

Posttest, page 133

3 three
8 eight
4 four
6 six
slide flip turn

Posttest, page 134

6, 8
5, 6
2, 1

Final Test

page 135

8	12	11	10	8	5
15	17	5	9	16	3
7	14	12	6	4	9
1	18	14	13	2	7
10	7	10	17	15	0
9	4	10	16	8	14
12	13	6	5	7	8

page 136

9	8	9	6	1	3
7	8	2	4	8	2
4	6	7	3	1	9
0	9	7	6	1	2
6	7	1	9	0	3
3	2	8	4	4	9
6	8	1	5	6	0

page 137

13¢
11
10
16¢
8
12

page 138

2¢
8
9
9¢
4
9

page 139

46¢	35¢
70¢	17¢
83¢	32¢
26¢	65¢
48¢	34¢

page 140

3
6
4